Chasing *the* Shadows:
Norfolk Mysteries Revisited

Chasing *the* Shadows:
Norfolk Mysteries Revisited

Bruce Robinson

Elmstead Publications
Wicklewood, Norfolk, NR18 9QL
Published 1996

© Bruce Robinson

Elmstead Publications, Elmstead, Milestone Lane, Wicklewood, Norfolk, NR18 9QL

First Published 1996

ISBN: 0 9523379 16

No part of this publication may be reproduced or transmitted in any form or by any means, electronic or mechanical, including photocopying, recording, or any information storage or retrieval system, without permission in writing from the author.

Text input and book design by the author using a DTP system with PageMaker 5. Main text font: Times New Roman.

Printed by Geo. Reeve Ltd, Wymondham, Norfolk.

Front cover picture by Bruce Robinson: statue of Boadicea, Westminster, London.

By the same author:

A History of Long Sutton (South Lincolnshire). Produced privately, 1965 (with F W Robinson).
The Peddars Way. The Weathercock Press, 1978.
A Skylark Descending (novel). Robert Hale, 1978.
History of Long Sutton & District. Long Sutton Civic Trust, 1981 (with F W Robinson). Reprinted 1995.
Norfolk Origins 1: Hunters to First Farmers. Acorn Editions, 1981 (with Andrew Lawson).
Norfolk Origins 2: Roads & Tracks. Poppyland Publishing, 1983 (with Edwin Rose).
The Peddars Way and Norfolk Coast Path. Countryside Commission, 1986.
Norfolk Origins 3: Celtic Fire & Roman Rule. Poppyland Publishing, 1987 (with Tony Gregory).
Peddars Way and Norfolk Coast Path. Aurum Press, 1992. Reprinted 1996.
Norfolk Fragments. Elmstead Publications, 1994.
A Glimpse of Distant Hills (novel). Elmstead Publications, 1995.

Foreword

AS an adopted son of Norfolk - 27 years here have just about given me that privilege - my lifelong fascination with history quickly developed into a passion for the historic past and architecture of this corner of England.

This is why my old friend Bruce Robinson's work in this field has always had a tremendous appeal. It is not only that Bruce writes with the spare momentum of a journalist and storyteller, which gives every panorama he recreates a vivid, living quality. He is at the same time an assiduous harvester of facts and detail who presents them skilfully as evidence, setting them out so that they speak for themselves and reveal their own pictures. Not for him the easy options of "probably," "possibly" or "must have been."

Take his account in this book of King John's legendary loss of his treasure in The Wash. The collection of evidence is painstaking and meticulous, the conclusions solid and convincing. Yet it is told with the pace and tension of a good detective tale of which Ellis Peters' Brother Cadfael would have approved.

As we survey the subject matter within this latest book from the Robinson pen, we begin with the comfortable confidence that we already have a pretty good working knowledge not only of King John and his treasure, but of Snettisham and its remarkable finds; of Boudica and her mighty fight against the Roman invaders; of Kett's Rebellion and its roots, causes and ramifications. But as we read on through the engrossing narrative we have the excitement of realising just how much more there is to know, and how reliable a guide we have upon our journey of discovery.

In this book we have local history as it should be: accurate as far as scholarship will allow, allied with a splendidly readable narrative style - and all brought together with a committed enthusiasm which is contagious.

From the earliest times the geography of Norfolk put it out on a limb, and allowed to develop here a sturdy individuality. Even today both these characteristics are still with us. It is a county in which the "native born" have a keen pride in the past and in their present. It is all these qualities, no doubt, which make "furriners" like me, who have made their homes here, become even more passionate and protective of Norfolk heritage than even the "locals" themselves.

It is the beauty of Bruce Robinson's book that it will appeal equally to both camps.

Charles Roberts
Yaxham, June 1996

Contents

Introduction

1: *The* Golden Coast, page 1

2: Queen *of* Shadows, page 14

3: Road *to* Nowhere, page 36

4: Lost *in the* Wash, page 60

5: *The* Great Commotion, page 77

Introduction

WHAT sort of mystery? As far as this book is concerned it has nothing to do with crime or crime detection. It discusses historical questions. And why these? Simply because they are mysteries which have intrigued me over the years, largely through some indirect association or other.

I was born and brought up in South Lincolnshire, a few miles from the old Wash estuary, so the story of King John and his jewels was familiar at a very early age. In Norwich, in the 1960s and 1970s, we lived in the hilly suburb of Thorpe Hamlet, the very area where Robert Kett had his Great Camp, and only yards from the ruins of St Michael's chapel. Again, walking holidays on the Peddars Way set me wondering why this particular Roman road was built, and why there was once a famous Iron Age precious metal industry in the vicinity.

As for the chapter on Boudica I must lay the blame, if blame there must be, at the door of the late Tony Gregory, an archaeologist who is greatly missed. On the final day of what for him had been an unusually long and difficult excavation at Thetford's curious Fison Way/Gallows Hill site, and while awaiting the arrival of the heavy machinery which was to fill in the holes and level the area, Tony took me on a last walk along the line of the (presumed) processional way, through the (possible) main entrance, and into the great, circular (probable) temple area. No trace of Boudica had been found but I felt then, and still feel, she must have walked that very same path at least once. In any event, I was hooked.

It must be emphasised I have undertaken no original research and have thus leaned heavily on the research and writings of others. I offer them all my thanks and point out that, where possible, I have acknowledged and listed their references and writings; the errors, incidentally, are mine. What I have tried to do is pull together some of the many available strands of information and theory and re-tell each tale as plainly and simply as I can. Here and there, and particularly in the chapters dealing with the Peddars Way and King John, I have taken the liberty of adding a few thoughts of my own.

At the end of each chapter you will find a brief bibliography and a list of places to visit or things to see. References in the text to an author, given without title or publisher, mean the details can be found at the end of the chapter. None of these lists are exhaustive and in at least two cases (Chapters 1 and 2) there are no proper related sites to visit. Some of the listed books deal with the subject being discussed only in passing, or perhaps in one chapter, and one or two titles, being elderly, may be to difficult trace.

Most of the photographs are mine; those that are not are labelled in the caption. The diagrammatic maps are all my own work and none are drawn to a proper scale.

This book represents my third attempt at self-publication, and once again I would like to thank those who have helped smooth the technical (ie, computer) bumps, in particular the staff of Geo. Reeve Ltd of Wymondham. Thanks are also due to the Editor of the Eastern Daily Press for his permission to use certain photographs from the EDP library. And my special thanks to Charles Roberts for agreeing to write the Foreword. Before I retired, Charles was an EDP colleague of many years standing, and there is little doubt that his extensive writing (theatre, books, columnist, food and drink) represents a literary bulwark in uncertain times.

Bruce Robinson

For over 40 years archaeological finds of objects of extraordinary beauty and significance have been unearthed in a field on a gently sloping hillside near Snettisham, in North West Norfolk, and in the vicinity. Following yet another huge find in 1990 and a subsequent British Museum excavation of the site, it is now realised that what has become known as the Snettisham Treasure represents the largest collection of Celtic and Iron Age torcs ever found in Europe. But it is still not known for certain what the collection represents, why it was buried, or even why this corner of the county housed such an obvious expression of great wealth.

1: *The* Golden Coast

In some small book or other, now lost or at least partially erased from memory, I once came across a reference to a local legend of some golden gates. This was several years ago and I have forgotten the essence of the tale, but I do recollect the story was said to have been associated with West and North West Norfolk, and by particular implication, with the Icknield Way.

Having long since mislaid the reference I have, of course, also forgotten my first reaction, but I am quite certain that I would, at worst, have connected the tale with the over-wrought imagination of a Victorian writer or even with gorse and broom bushes which burgeon in gorgeous yellow and gold profusion on the light, sandy soils in spring and early summer; and at best put the legend down to a faint folk recollection of passing Celtic trade and Druidic gold being shipped across country through Norfolk to the coast.

But the slight praise of yesterday needs tempering, today, with caution. If that same story was recorded before, should we say, 1947, then it certainly deserves fresh consideration. The fact of the matter is that a small, arable field on the slopes of Ken Hill, near Snettisham, has been known locally as the Treasure or Gold Field since 1948 and has subsequently become world famous, and for very obvious reasons. At the very least, its place among the pages of Norfolk's history is assured.

Ken Hill, an obvious landmark when viewed from the sea, is a tree-smothered knuckle of land which rises suddenly and almost unexpectedly out of the shore. But this is a story which stems originally from a simple post-war agricultural decision to switch a farm crop from lavender to barley, and in the process, to have a particular field deep ploughed. It was the fashion of the time, a system developed during the war years when, for the sake of expediency and extra food, and because of labour shortages, the tractor hastened the end of the reign of the horse as the main power source on the land. Deep ploughing also sent archaeologists of the day into spasms of excitement just as metal detecting, for all its many contentious side issues and shady possibilities, and even greater results, was to do a few decades later.

However, at Snettisham in the late autumn of 1948 such matters were not even on the horizon. Here, the carrstone is about a foot beneath the soil, and it was the custom with horses not to go much deeper than about seven inches. This time, using a tractor, it was to be ploughed in 12in furrows.

Farm worker Ray Williamson, then 23, was given the task, and when at some point his plough snagged what he thought were bits of a brass bedstead he stopped, untangled the debris, and left the pieces in a heap at the edge of the furrow. Afterwards, he showed them to his farm foreman. Two days later his tractor and plough unearthed more fragments of what looked like twisted wire and some small discs. This time a local member of the Norfolk Research Committee correctly identified the items as Iron Age torcs, and quite naturally alerted the authorities. Then the first excavation was carried out, by R Rainbird Clarke, who uncovered two hollows containing scrap metal, coins and iron nails, perhaps from wooden boxes which may have contained the metals.

Inevitably, the subject of a treasure trove inquest arose, and a coroner's jury sitting in Hunstanton was finally called upon to decide if the objects had been hidden and if the original owner could not be traced, in which case the collection would be declared treasure trove; or if the treasure was lost or abandoned without thought of recovery. The nicety of the law on this particular subject was as complicated and pedantic then as now. In the event the jury decided on the former, and the torcs were duly "seized" by the coroner on behalf of the Crown.

Farsightedly, that same jury - which included only one woman, I believe - also recommended that the hoard be kept together. The precious pieces were duly taken to Norwich Castle Museum.

It was evidently the custom a mere 20 years or so before this date that such finds went unrewarded, but in the 1930s the Treasury and the British Museum, mindful that there was precious little incentive to hand in such treasures and discoveries and that items were probably being lost, agreed a payments formula.

And so a few months after the initial discovery the tractor driver received a cheque for £400. The owner of the land on which the discovery had been made received nothing.

The archaeologists who scoured the field and found a few more bits and pieces also missed - by 15ft, so it was said later - a second major discovery. In November, 1950, another tractor driver, Tom Rout, ploughing in the same area, unearthed a torc, and a week later, brought a second torc to the surface. The first weighed 2lb 2oz. The second, a monster which tipped the scales at 3lb 7oz, subsequently became known as the Great Torc.

A truly wonderful object, it was made of 64 separate strands of twisted gold. Inside one of the decorated terminal ends British Museum conservation staff found an Iron Age coin, presumably inserted for luck or to correct a weight imbalance.

Tom Rout and the Great Torc. Picture: Eastern Daily Press.

Seven months later Mr Rout received his reward, a cheque for £1850, while the owner once again went empty handed, as it were. This cheque represented a great deal of money at a time when wages stood at about £5 a week, and the matter sparked an esoteric debate, one writer (A J Forrest. Under Three Crosses. The Boydell Press, 1961) commenting a year or two later: "The effect of such gifts upon a small working community should be carefully weighed. Local dissatisfaction may easily arise from it."

Quite how wide and intense the debate was, or how deep the local dissatisfaction, I do not know. In any event there were other things to talk about, for in 1964, 1968, and again in 1973, there were more discoveries.

At this point there seems to have been a feeling among experts that the best had been and gone and that the site had largely been destroyed by continuous farming operations, and for a number of years things went quiet. Then in 1989/90 came the big one. Metal detector user Cecil Hodder, who had permission to explore the site, literally struck gold.

This time the size and scale of the find was awesome, and this time, too, in a painstaking response mounted at great speed and in an atmosphere of secrecy - not all metal detector users being made of the right stuff - staff from the British Museum carefully combed three acres of land. Using highly sophisticated techniques they garnered a huge haul of 112 more complete or fragmented torcs, over 100 gold or silver alloy ingots, and more than 170 coins.

In all, nearly 180 torcs had now been recovered from Ken Hill, many having been buried in shallow pits cut into the carrstone. Thanks largely to the coins the depositions, at first thought to emanate from the 1st century AD, were dated to about 70BC, which positions some of the burials nearly a generation before Caesar's first scouting expeditions to Britain, roughly 30 years before the birth of Christ, and 90 years before a major tribal revolt brought Roman retribution crashing down on Norfolk heads.

There is little doubt now that the Gold Field has thoroughly earned its sobriquet while somehow managing to preserve its integrity and almost all of its mystery. Ken Hill has given up its untarnished treasure slowly and reluctantly; and that, of course, has simply added to the allure.

What were torcs, and were they set apart from our own experience? Apparently not. They seem to have been no more unusual than, or have their parallels in, the Crown Imperial, Lady So-and-so's tiara, a title, a religious icon, or even a Lonsdale Belt. They did essentially the same job.

On the continent in the 5th and 4th centuries BC, and particularly in the Champagne region, torcs were commonly of bronze and mostly worn by women. Later, Barbara Green points out, there is evidence that torcs became a part of warrior attire. In England, from the Bronze Age onwards they were worn with a flourish as symbols of wealth, prestige or authority, and sometimes no doubt as all three. They may also have had a religious significance. Celtic warriors certainly wore them, and according to Dio Cassius even Boudica, the great queen (see Chapter 2), sported a "great gold neck ring." It also seems likely some torcs had a ritual function and adorned Celtic statues of gods and goddesses, and wood and stone idols, perhaps being worn in public only on State occasions or at a time of war.

More precisely, torcs - a form of spelling I prefer to torque, which always seems to me to contain engineering overtones, but which is actually Latin for "necklace," derived in turn from torquere, meaning "to twist" - were heavy rings of precious metal, sometimes gold, sometimes silver, sometimes copper, but more often than not of electrum, which is a composite. Generally, the method of construction was to take wires, or bars, twist them together, and add highly decorated ends.

The GOLDEN COAST

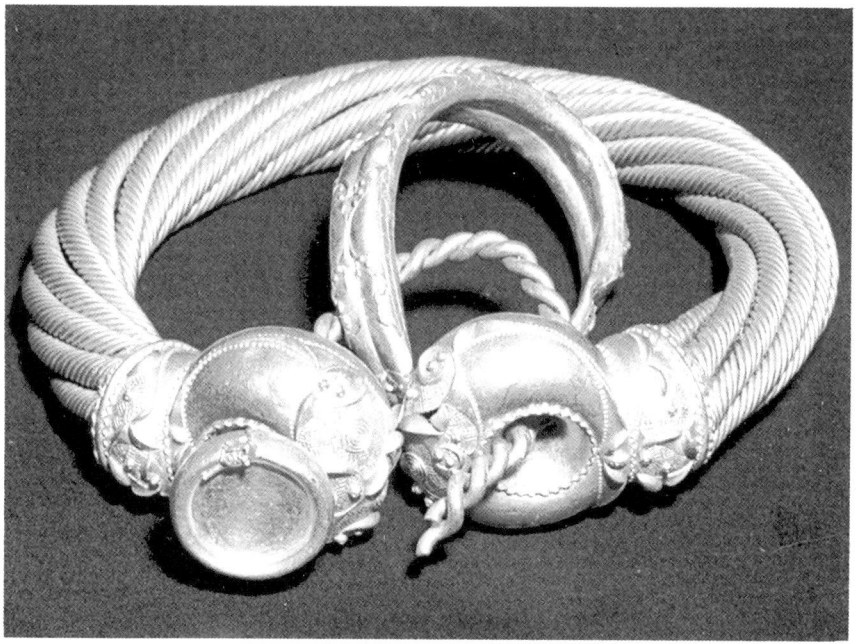

The beautiful Great Torc. Picture: Eastern Daily Press.

So they were expensive and they were worn by gods, royalty and by warriors, male and female, all of which leads to the next question. Did the wearing of a torc make someone special, or was the torc a reward for specialness? A mixture of both, no doubt.

But despite the mystique and the symbolistic overtones, there was also something very human about them. Those in the know, those who, overcome by curiosity or possibly even in the pursuit of knowledge, have actually coiled one around their neck, report them to be heavy, stiff, cold, unwieldy and seriously uncomfortable. Most generations, it seems, were and are prepared to suffer for fashion.

There are other factors to keep in mind about the Snettisham torcs, one being that because of their intrinsic value they may also have been used as currency or seen as units of wealth. In effect, and despite their weight and awkwardness, they may have been used as high demonination "bank notes" particularly before coinage was in widespread use. The Iceni, it seems, did not trade for Mediterranean goods as other tribes in the south-east did, and may therefore have retained many of their torcs.

Other factors include quality and culture. Today's auction houses dealing in high art play on very similar emotions and cultivate financial values by working along very similar lines. Indeed, to put the matter into some sort of monetary framework, one estimate of the precious metal value of the 1990 hoard from Ken Hill suggests it would have been worth 40,000 to 50,000 denarii to Caesar, which would have had a purchasing power at today's rates of between four and five million pounds. Some torcs are undoubtedly major works of art. Their real value on today's open market - perhaps double that sum - cannot be tested.

As for Ken Hill, no related site evidence was found of metal working or of nearby habitation, but Late Bronze Age pottery fragments were discovered and coin scatters indicate some sort of industrial activity for a generation or so after the burials, which may or may not have taken place all at the same time.

In any event the burials themselves were curious. Many of the pieces were in closely packed "nests," each hoard being in a small pit hewn out of the carrstone underlying the fields. One pit was filled with 50 neck rings, 70 bracelets and a few coins. One torc, originally squeezed to fit a tiny pit, actually sprang back into its original shape immediately it was lifted out by excavators. Another, old and much-repaired when buried, might possibly have dated from the 3rd century BC.

Some pits were deeper than others, and there was evidently a slight suggestion that the more precious torcs had been given special, meaning deeper, protection. Many of the coins were damaged or unfinished or chopped in two. Analysis of some of the gold suggested it had been recycled many times.

The immediate, overall impression was that the collection represented the stock-in-trade of an unknown smith - torcs in states of disrepair, bits and pieces awaiting recycling, and coins which might be melted down for their precious metal content.

A major surprise for the excavators, however, was the discovery nearby of traces of a 20-acre ditched enclosure, with one entrance, which seemed to encircle the area. It had been dug when the landscape was open and covered with grass and bracken. Later, during the Roman occupation, the ditches had been filled in using, among other material, slag and furnace debris. Embedded in the latter were fragments of charcoal which gave a date of 10bc (radiocarbon), plus or minus 80 years.

The enclosure has puzzled archaeologists, and it must be said the debate goes on. Did it actually define the hoard area and therefore have some particular symbolic or ownership significance? Possibly. Was it defensive, in a military sense? Almost certainly not.

Perhaps it was a combination of the two in that its mystery, and an invented reputation, was sufficient to keep people away. After all, the reputation of Grim kept generations of Brecklanders at arms length from Grimes Graves, or at least sufficiently eroded memories for folk to have forgotten what the "graves" actually were and then to have re-invented them as a ubiquitous "Danish encampment."

The mystery of Ken Hill, near Snettisham.

Clearly, ghostly associations work. And despite the presence of a villa only a short distance away, the Romans seem never to have found the field of gold.

To begin to consider some of the implications of the hoard it is necessary to return to the Middle and Late Bronze Ages when supplies of metals from Britain and the continent, along with recycled scrap, enabled itinerant smiths to produce vast quantities of artefacts. One of these metal working areas may have been Snettisham and Sedgeford, which would therefore have been a metal working centre of very long standing.

In any event the industrious Late Bronze Age smiths, perhaps working a particular area or route, seem to have buried some of their stock with the intention of digging it up again next time they were in the vicinity. Dozens of caches of these stocks-in-trade have been discovered which, when studied, evidently indicate a warrior-based society in which this particular industry may have been centrally controlled.

Why were so many bronze hoards discarded, abandoned, forgotten? First, gold happened, reaching the area about 1100BC, after which the first torcs appeared. More significantly, iron also happened, in about 650BC.

Iron provided a better and more dependable cutting edge than bronze, so redundant and unfashionable stock was left in the ground for the plough and the metal detector to discover. In addition, some low grade ores also became available, including those of the Greensand deposits of West Norfolk. Iron working settlements have been found not only at Snettisham but also in the Setchey and Blackborough End areas, perhaps with resident smiths supplying swords and spearheads, billhooks and sickles to local farms and families.

The distribution of Iron Age sites and finds in West Norfolk shows clear concentrations in the Snettisham and Heacham areas, while an arc of Iron Age forts running from the coast and as far south as the Icknield Way crossing of the river Thet, seems to have marked out or protected essentially the same region.

Warham fort, a formidable structure, once had a wooden palisade and fighting platform; Holkham fort, surrounded by marshes, sits on the tip of a curving sand spit; South Creake, now ploughed out but still detectable as a crop mark, is thought to have been the largest Iron Age fort in Norfolk; Narborough, close to the Icknield Way and the crossing of the Nar, had huge banks of chalk rubble; while Thetford, which also guarded a river crossing, was so prominent and conveniently-placed that it was converted by the Normans into a motte and bailey castle.

Whether built as private statements or out of some sort of community need, the forts certainly look as though they stand guard over landward and river approaches to the chalk uplands, and in consequence, over the scattered farmsteads of West and North West Norfolk.

During the 1st century BC the area around Snettisham and Hunstanton, safely tucked inside the arc, may well have been a tribal centre or the home of the ruling royal family with the powerful elite, one assumes, expressing themselves in outward displays of wealth in the form of personal adornment and ornate horse and chariot harness and trappings.

The area, or at least the controlling portion of the population, was indeed wealthy, for torcs have been found not only at Snettisham and Sedgeford, but also at North Creake, Bawsey, Middleton, and possibly Fincham and Weybourne.

It was during the 1st century BC, too, that coins first began to be used in Britain, most of them gold, though Norfolk tribes, doing different as usual, seem to have been a little late on the uptake.

Interestingly, one hoard of gold Iron Age coins found in the area, dating from about the same period as the Snettisham torcs, may have been hoarded purposely to be melted down and recycled into torcs. Either gold supplies were being squeezed or this was another touch of local individuality. Tribal communities outside Norfolk seem to have kept gold coins in general circulation; in Norfolk, which was geographically isolated and which retained many Celtic and Belgic influences, it is possible such coins were valued simply for their gold content and kept for conversion into torcs.

Then something strange happened. Iceni coin finds tend to begin to concentrate in the south of the region, suggesting that for some reason or another there was a shift in economic and political emphasis and that by the 1st century AD the tribal focus had moved to the Brecks and the Thetford area, or even east towards Caistor St Edmund, which ultimately became a Roman controlled tribal capital.

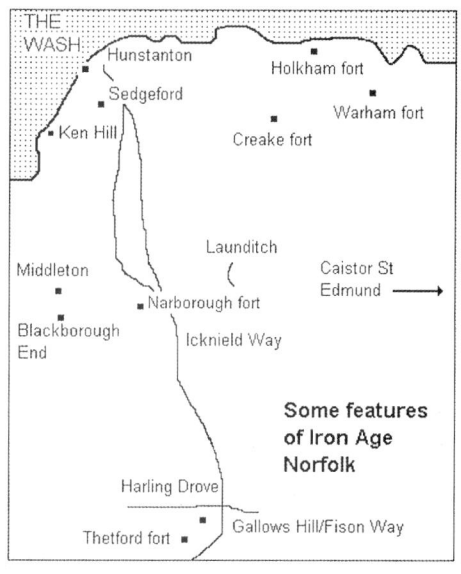

Some features of Iron Age Norfolk

The discovery of a massive and mysterious site at Fison Way/Gallows Hill, on high ground above Thetford, also lends weight to the southward drift theory. Between 200 and 100BC there was a small farming settlement at Fison Way, but in about AD30 an imposing double-ditch enclosure was built surrounding three large timber round houses. A few years later a third ditch was dug and the area between the new and earlier ditches filled with row upon row of huge timber fences.

Again, any defensive intent has been ruled out despite the fact that the Romans seem to have dismantled it. Perhaps they simply needed the timber. A balance of opinion has it that this was a site of major ceremonial and tribal significance.

Despite a great deal of uncertainty and no precise dating for any of the Norfolk's Iron Age forts, it is possible to drawn up a sketchy sort of timetable, thus:

Circa 1100BC. Smiths working in Norfolk. Gold reaches the area and first torcs eventually appear.

Circa 650BC. The first iron arrives in Norfolk.

Circa 100BC. Roman trading links established with the South Coast, Essex and the Thames Estuary, but Norfolk largely bypassed or ignored. The first coins, mainly gold, appear in Britain.

1st century BC. There seems to have been a major tribal focal point in West Norfolk, perhaps in the Snettisham and Sedgeford area. Precious metal smiths working in the area and high quality torcs being produced.

Circa 70BC. The Snettisham Treasure burials.

Circa 55 and 54BC. Caesar's scouting expeditions to Britain.

Circa 15BC. First local coins produced.

Circa AD1 to 47. Tribal economic and political focal point drifts south to Thetford and the Brecks and east towards Caistor St Edmund.

Circa AD30 to AD59. Small settlement at Fison Way, Thetford, gradually altered and developed into a large and unusual ceremonial centre.

Circa AD60. Later Roman writers say Boudica wore a torc around her neck.

It is surely safe to assume that from the moment Roman and Celtic traders first made contact with each other the word "gold" figured in their commercial deliberations. Certainly Tacitus, writing several decades after the Boudiccan Revolt, acknowledged the metal had a major part in determining Roman strategy. "Britain," he wrote, "yields gold, silver and other metals, to make it worth conquering." Even its crops, though slow to ripen, were quick to grow.

Of course, he wrote from the position of a conqueror and displayed a conqueror's viewpoint, adding deliciously: "Who the first inhabitants of Britain were, whether natives or immigrants, remains obscure; one must remember we are dealing with barbarians." He probably meant strange or foreign rather than savage, but the gist of his comment remains important. To the Romans, the British were a very odd lot.

Even so, it is pertinent to remember that despite a knowledge of British gold industries, and despite nearby estate villas, extensive community and agricultural operations over the centuries, local knowledge and folklore, and the proximity of travellers on the Icknield Way, these treasures, at least, were never found. If the villa owners knew of the earthwork, as presumably they did, they must have left it largely unexplored. Ken Hill kept its own counsel. Perhaps ghostly implications impart a more powerful influence than we realise.

An interesting side issue is that over a century ago the Rev Scott F Surtees, rector of Sprotburgh, Yorkshire, produced a curious booklet (Julius Caesar: Did he cross the Channel? Smith, London, 1866) in which he firmly rejected the traditional view of Dover/Deal landings. Instead, he maintained in his quirky polemic that Caesar had sailed fom the mouths of the Rhine or the Scheldt, or possibly the foreshore of Walcheren, and landed between Brancaster and Cromer. According to a confident Mr Surtees the Romans then marched inland to Hanworth and engaged the locals in battle on the banks of the Glaven river.

However, to return to the main subject. Important questions are left in the wake. Many of the Snettisham Treasure items seem to have been buried as caches of scrap, bullion and spare parts. Some items were battered and bent and evidently ready to be melted down for re-use.

During the lst century BC in particular the gold and silver smiths of the Snettisham and Sedgeford area produced great numbers of torcs, perhaps to special order, and exported them all over Britain. For example, Snettisham's expertise - the manufacture of torcs seems to have been an Iceni speciality - has been identified in torcs found at several places including Clevedon (Somerset), Needwood Forest (Staffordshire), Ulceby (Lincolnshire) and Netherud (Peebles). Traders, or a Druidic hierarchy, could have transported them inland using the Icknield Way, or perhaps shipped them to the continent from a Norfolk port. It is at least possible that Ken Hill was once connected to an inlet from the Wash.

The salient point is that Snettisham craftsmanship was of the highest possible order. The workers' artistry and expertise was much prized and in great demand. Thus they were people of influence with reputations which spread wider than the boundaries of the modern county.

Today, these unknown folk would be acknowledged as masters of their craft. Instead, a fog of unknowing descends. Was it one man? Was it a workshop? Was it a group following a classical design tradition? These are secrets the hill keeps within its ken and ones we may never strip bare.

There also remains the questions of why the hoard was buried and what it actually represents, and it must be said there are almost as many theories as there are torcs. The main ones are summarised here.

A religious or votive deposit. The presence of an enclosure lends weight to this line of thinking, but there is evidently no precedent for it. Known Iron Age religious depositions have tended to be in bogs or rivers, and none of those have included a torc. Also, archaeologists have not so far come across any grave, temple, sacred grove or even a sign of habitation at Ken Hill.

The hoard was buried at a time of danger. There is no evidence to support the idea and the enclosure was apparently not built for defence. But it is always possible there was tribal unrest or internal strife at the time, or neighbours who had become a threat.

A cache awaiting shipment. The hoard evidently has more of the feel of scrap and bullion about it than the actual finished article, though of course that does not demolish the theory entirely. Another problem is that it is not known how deeply the "nests" or artefacts were originally buried.

It was a tribal, family, or even workshop-owned bullion repository. There were no banks or building societies, so the burial of valued items was one of the few genuine options. But uncertainties persist. The overall value of the metals suggests it is too rich a hoard for a single craftsman; this was not the stock-in-trade of an ordinary smith. If tribal, then it raises the prospect of an early Iceni palace in the Snettisham and Hunstanton area still awaiting discovery. And Ken

Hill's position towards the north-western end of the Icknield Way - a name which may derive from the Celtic tribal name, Iceni - lends strength to this idea. On the other hand if it was tribal, and given the longevity of communal memory, why was it never recovered? And did the enclosure actually mark out the bullion area, or was it dug out at some other time?

The tribal bank theory remains the most compelling, but until more is understood about Ken Hill we can only stand back from the Snettisham Treasure and look in awe at the workmanship.

In essence, the past is silent and some things we shall never know, which is how it should be. But whatever the truth, Ken Hill and the nameless people who once worked there, or nearby, have earned their niche in Norfolk history, and the phantom of a forgotten Faberge or an unknown Benvenuto Cellini continues to haunt the furrowed and mysterious tree-lined slopes of Ken Hill.

The Icknield Way near Swaffham.

LATE ADDENDUM: The reference in the introduction to a local legend of golden gates was included in a newspaper article by C H Lewton-Brain (EDP, July 14, 1977). Folklore, he said, claimed that some golden gates were buried in a field near Heacham. He also said a field at Flitcham, near Sandringham, was once called Drakenhowe, or Dragon's Hill. The job of dragons, he added, was to guard treasure in a burial ground.

SELECTED REFERENCES AND READING

Davies, Gregory, Lawson, Rickett and Rogerson. The Iron Age Forts of Norfolk. (EAA 54). East Anglian Archaeology, 1992.

Dymond, David. The Norfolk Landscape. Hodder & Stoughton, 1985.
Fraser, Antonia. Boadicea's Chariot. Weidenfeld & Nicholson, 1985.
Frere, Sheppard. Britannia. Pimlico, 1987.
Green, Barbara. Iron Age Torcs (article). The Quarterly, No 18. Norfolk Archaeological and Historical Research Group, 1995.
Gregory, Tony. Excavations in Thetford, 1980-1982, Fison Way, Volume 1. (EAA 53). East Anglian Archaeology, 1992.
Megaw & Megaw. Celtic Art. Thames & Hudson, 1989.
Robinson and Gregory. Celtic Fire and Roman Rule. Poppyland, 1987.
Tacitus. On Britain and Germany. Translated by H. Mattingly. Penguin, 1948.
Williamson, Tom. The Origins of Norfolk. Manchester University Press, 1993.
Wade-Martins, Peter. An Historical Atlas of Norfolk. Norfolk Museums Service, 1993.

PLACES TO VISIT

Castle Museum, Norwich, has a display and a great deal of information on the Snettisham Treasure. Here you can see some of the torcs, originals and replicas, at close quarters.
The Iron Age fort at Warham, near Wells, just off the Wighton-Warham road. There is a great sense of atmosphere about the place.
The British Museum, London.

> *The story of Boudica, East Anglia's own Warrior Queen, is one of a woman in the shadows. She is universally seen as our first real national heroine, as one who came within a spear's throw of changing the course of this country's history. Yet not a single known artefact can be described as having belonged to her, not a single Norfolk site said to have been in her personal domain. All there is to go on are some sparse references which relate only to the last few months of her life and which were written years later by Roman historians, and a little archaeological evidence which seems to support the texts. Despite this, the story of Boudica and the Revolt against Rome is recognised by every school child in the land. We may not know her, but her life has cast long shadows.*

2: Queen *of* Shadows

For many decades it was a cornerstone of historical teaching that every school child, and particularly every Norfolk school child, should absorb at least a brief outline of the Boudican Revolt against Rome. Even in South Lincolnshire where I was born the rule held good. Thus somewhere within the general category of Ancient Britons we studied line drawings and colour wash representations as the story unfolded. And what a story! Chariots and heroism, the clash of sword on shield, the rallying of the Iceni against the hated invader; and death, bravely met. It was glory in defeat, a story of our time, an epic episode of Dunkirk proportions.

Over the years this has been the repeated theme. Cruelty perpetuated by the invader, local resentment, rebellion and death. The wronged Queen of Norfolk pitted against the military might of Rome. Perhaps it helps to explain why she is buried so deep in the regional psyche. But the fact remains that the episode was infinitely more complex than any brief outline can suggest, and many times more fascinating. Coincidence and politics, military planning and insane recklessness, personalities, opportunity, hard experience and sudden inspiration, all played a part in what was a key episode in British history.

True, the image of the Warrior Queen still dominates the stage, just as Thomas Thorneycroft's spirited bronze statue of Boadicea (the official, presumably Victorian spelling) and her daughters, erected beside Westminster Bridge in London in 1902, somehow captures the essence of the legend. But reality and subsequent discoveries have blurred the edges. The episode was not as clear-cut as the summary would have us believe; her chariot did not have knives on its wheels; and the final episodes of the drama were played out against the backcloth of an orgy of bloodletting.

What does remain intact is the achievement. The fact is that Boudica did come within an ace of ending Roman rule in Britain. For a few short weeks Nero's army in Britannia, the land at the edge of the known world, hovered on the brink of disaster. Years of history and all its legacies, many of which survive to this day, could so easily have been changed forever.

Had she succeeded, you and I would have been living in a very different sort of land and a different sort of society. Thus whatever the image we continue to carry the reality remains large and potent. Boudica, the first named and first faintly discernible Norfolk woman to emerge from the mists of time, has earned her place in the history books.

The actual events are more difficult to relate, the basic problem being the paucity of evidence. Ask any pupil what Boudica did and he or she will tell you. Ask an archaeologist who she was, where she came from, where she lived, or indeed for any sort of detail to clothe the bones of her personal story, and they will demur. In fact, ask any expert to point to anything, or any site, which has a positively identified connection with Boudica and you will stare exasperation in the face.

Despite much study, many books and a great deal of investigative digging she remains a largely unknown factor, a woman who stepped from the shadows, did her deed and stepped back again. More precisely, all that is known of her comes courtesy of brief references by Romans - the enemy, remember - generally written second-hand many years after the period in question, and which in any event relate to only a few of the events which occurred during one short period in the final year of her life. The rest is silence.

Such is the potency of the tale. Before we attempt to lift at least a part of the veil, however, it is necessary to take two decisions, over the contentious and much-argued issues of the spelling of Boudica and the circa AD60 date of the revolt of the Iceni. I accept both, purely on the grounds that at the time of writing they seem to hold general, if not complete, acceptance. Boudica and AD60 it is.

Late Bronze Age/Iron Age transition sites have been identified in Breckland and near Hunstanton, and find-spot maps tend to confirm that most early Iron Age sites and metalworking areas (see Chapter 1) were concentrated in the west of the county, around the Fen edge, the Greensand belt, and Breckland, most notably on the lighter and drier soils.

In the days before coinage was in general use in Norfolk a great deal of Iron Age business was carried out by barter, precious metals (gold, silver) being traded for ornaments and jewellery and iron for tools and weapons. The problem was to establish some sort of accepted standard, and there is evidence that one solution was the distribution of iron currency bars, shaped like the blade of a sword, which actually contained enough iron to make a sword. Standards for gold and silver were similarly established by marks which presumably guaranteed weight and purity and which were stamped on the metals by the issuing authority.

When the Iceni did begin somewhat belatedly to produce their own gold stater coins their appearance was similar to those already put into circulation by their neighbours, the Catuvellauni, north of the Thames, and the Trinovantes of Essex.

During the middle Iron Age period the Iceni - whose origins may be hidden in earlier folk movements from Belgium and Holland, arrivals who could have made landfall on the shores of the Wash or along Norfolk's rivers - seem to have begun to drift inland and away from the Fen edges. Even so they did not stray far, staying mostly in the west of the county and continuing to avoid the heavy clay soils.

Clearly there was some territorial concern, a digging in, for some experts feel that the Launditch, Panworth Ditch, Birchamditch and Fossditch may belong to this phase. Certainly the Launditch (Andrew Rogerson, article, Bulletin No 4, Norfolk Archaeological and Historical Research Group, 1995) was overlain by a later Roman road, and Tom Williamson (The Origins of Norfolk. Manchester University Press, 1993) has suggested it may have represented a frontier between the Iceni and one of the obscure tribes mentioned by Caesar. Williamson also pointed out that further linear earthworks could have existed. Another, also called the "Laundyche" and evidently mentioned in medieval documents, may have related to the Holme and Thornham areas near the seaward terminus of the later Roman road, the Peddars Way (see Chapter 3).

However, new developments in the field of agriculture and a booming population ultimately allowed or forced the horse loving Iceni to spread right across the county and certainly well beyond a defensive arc of the early forts (Tasburgh excepting, as this construction apparently relates to the post-Roman period, probably around AD900).

Other things happened, too. The Iceni seem to have switched from gold to silver to make their coins. Perhaps they needed the gold for their torcs; perhaps supplies fluctuated or the value changed. At the same time coins bearing the unified name Ecen - which may be the name of a ruler rather than another version of Iceni - dated roughly to the AD43-61 period, underpin the idea that at about this time a number of disparate groups fused together to become one.

It is difficult to perceive what did happen, and when. But a weight of evidence suggests that there were originally tribal sub-divisions and that, for some reason, the groups moved closer together, perhaps in some sort of political federation. In any event the kingdom of the horse, a single tribe of the Iceni, cannot really be perceived until about 50 years before the Roman conquest.

The picture which emerges thereafter is one of local wealth (for a select social class, no doubt), fertile fields, healthy herds and population growth. It also seems they had precious little to do with the Roman traders spreading out from operating bases on the south coast, or with their representatives. At least, the Iceni do not seem to have craved or sought the latest fashions and innovations from abroad. Interestingly, some late Iron Age settlements including Spong Hill (near North Elmham), Eaton Heath (Norwich), Crownthorpe (near Wymondham) and Threxton (near Watton) did continue into the Roman period, but the over-riding impression that remains is of a territory and a people who were proud, colourful, aloof, independent and largely self supporting. It can be argued, of course, that this is where some of the characteristics of modern Norfolk people come from.

Amanda Chadburn has pointed out that some 65 Iceni coin types are now known, "typified by their vigorous Celtic stylised designs which often include animals, and symbols which might be cosmological ones, suns, moons and stars." Some of the early silver coins were inscribed.

In AD25-30 the names Cans and Dvro appeared, perhaps abbreviations of two joint rulers. From about AD30-50 Anted, or Antedios, may have ruled, while in the AD50s the single names Saenu and Aesu seem to have been among those who held some sort of sway. Then, and from about the same period, a new name was discovered, unearthed among a coin hoard found at Joist Fen, Lakenheath - Subriprasto (Prasto?), or Prasutagus. More recently another coin hoard later dated to circa AD60, with one of the coins bearing the legend Subriprasto Esico Fecit, was discovered at Fincham (Norfolk Archaeology. Vol XL11, part 2, 1995). The wide gulf in the spelling is not all that surprising. Prasutagus is known only from coinage and from the writings of Roman historians who used Latin versions (perhaps phonetic) of a Celtic name told to them by others who had searched their memories for details of events years before.

Evidence of late Iron Age occupation of an area near the Roman town of Caistor St Edmund (Venta Icenorum) has also been discovered just outside of the north wall. Find spots of Boudican period silver coin hoards also tend to radiate out from Caistor (and from Thetford and Threxton), and even though no habitation site has so far been uncovered at Caistor it does suggest there may have been a major late Iron Age tribal centre near the confluence of the rivers Yare and Tas - an area much scarred by the recently constructed Norwich southern bypass - and that it may have been a focal point of the revolt of AD60.

In 55BC Caesar's ships scouted the island. He must have known a great deal about it even before the expedition, for there had been a tradition of trading with Gaul for many years and Roman entrepreneurs no doubt furnished him with some idea of what lay in store. In any event he did not stay long, but he did return the following year, perhaps in a move designed to impress the locals with Roman might and thus dissuade the Belgae in Britain from lending assistance to Gaulish cousins in their struggle against Rome. The effect of his reappearance was certainly dramatic, for five tribes promptly sent delegations to sue for peace. Four of them - the Segontiaci, Ancalites, Bibroci and Cassi - promptly disappear from the stage of history. A fifth was the Cenimagni, which may have been a faction of the Iceni. After all, if the Ceni was the Great Iceni, then there may have been a Lesser or even a Little Iceni.

Caesar must have been delighted, and he may have offered military protection. The fact of the matter was that Cassivellaunus and the Catuvellauni people had, in the words of Tony Gregory, "turned bullish again." The Cenimagni (or Iceni?) may have felt their territory was under threat. In any event, they seem to have declined to join a Catuvellaunian alliance against the invaders. Perhaps it was

An Iron Age reconstruction at Cockley Cley.

this refusal that riled Cassivellaunus in the first place. Other tribes had also felt threatened by the Catuvellauni for a stream of pro-Roman British kings and politicians had travelled to Rome to implore the emperors to intervene.

The delegations did not have much luck. Augustus and Tiberius largely ignored the pleadings of the bothersome Britons. Caesar's two visits, therefore, may have been prudently timed and useful. At least he now knew there was a pro-Roman bloc opposed to the restless and war-like Catuvellauni.

In AD39, some 93 years after Caesar's last visit, the insane Caligua finally assembled an army and a fleet at Boulogne with the intention of mounting an invasion. The troops, fearful of the unknown, declined to embark. Two years later Caligua was murdered and replaced by his uncle, Claudius, who is seen as a scholar rather than a soldier and as an emperor in desperate need of a military victory to cement his precarious position. Perhaps he remembered the Boulogne debacle, and resolved to do better; perhaps Britannia represented a relatively weak target and an easy victory; or perhaps news reached him that the Catuvellauni had gone on the warpath again. Whatever the trigger, in AD43 another invasion force was assembled, this time under the command of Aulus Plautius. The news, when it finally filtered through, may even have come as a huge relief to some of the Iceni, who felt threatened.

When the force was finally unleashed about 50,000 fighting men, stores, animals and equipment, transported by a huge fleet, crossed the Channel, stormed ashore, brushed British resistance aside and swept across country to the Thames, where they paused for breath. The object, no doubt, was to allow the emperor his moment of glory. Of the two kings of the Catuvellauni (of Hertfordshire and Bedfordshire) and the Trinovantes (Essex and parts of Suffolk), Togodumnus was dead, Caractacus had fled west, and the anti-Roman alliance was in disarray. More, the old Trinovantian capital of Camulodunum (Colchester) lay before them. When Claudius arrived, with much pomp and possibly a few elephants, the army entered the city.

This time eleven British tribal chiefs submitted and Claudius had his triumph. In Norfolk - where the Iceni were to be granted favoured client kingdom status - a line of early Roman military forts were built at Swanton Morley, Threxton and Scole, and at Ixworth (Suffolk), perhaps to establish a military barrier between factions of the Iceni. In any event the Romans were now in control of most of south-east England.

They seem to have spent four years or so strengthening their grip and establishing garrisons. Then in AD47 or 48 came a rude awakening. Aulus Plautius, who later disappeared from the scene after his wife was evidently accused of observing "foreign superstitions," possibly Christianity, was replaced by Ostorius Scapula. He arrived with explicit instructions to complete the conquest of the islands. But it was easier said than done. Caractacus was still a large thorn in the Roman side, having brought together tribes in Wales and the west Midlands to resist the invasion and damage the invaders' cause.

With comparatively few troops at his disposal, and most of those spread over a wide area, Scapula had little option, in gathering together a plausible force, but to strip many of the scattered garrisons. When he did finally march west he left

An air of mystery at Warham Camp.

behind tracts of country largely bereft of soldiers hoping, no doubt, that most of the pro-Roman tribes of the south-east would remain friendly. But Scapula was a seasoned fighting man, unused to leaving anything to chance. To ensure the peace, therefore, he enacted the Roman law, the Lex Julia de Armis, which effectively disarmed conquered people. The effect was to strip all of the tribes of most of their weapons.

It was also a rude awakening for the Iceni - described by Tacitus, incidentally, as "a powerful nation (and) not yet broken in battle . . . " - most of whom had hitherto thought they were on friendly terms with the Romans. They, or some of the tribal groups, had formally submitted to Rome and had retained their tribal identity. They had a right to feel they could be trusted. Now a Roman was treating them like any other conquered people, and worse, attempting to disarm them. Not everyone accepted the indignity and some finally rose in revolt. Few details of the incident are known but it was, clearly, a military threat. With factions of the Iceni leading the way the anti-Roman elements, including groups from neighbouring tribes, among them the Coritani, withdrew into a stronghold of earth banks and ditches and with a single line of approach along a narrow entrance.

No doubt they thought they were safe. Having got used to the ways of Plautius, perhaps they wanted to test the mettle of the new man. If so, the plan was a spectacular failure. Scapula, with a force which included cavalry, ordered them to dismount, surrounded the fort with auxiliary infantry and stormed the stronghold on foot.

It is uncertain where this action took place, and it has to be admitted that the description does fit Holkham fort. Weight of opinion, though, places the incident at Stonea, near March, then a fortified island amid the peat Fens and surrounded by watercourses. But wherever it was the effect was the same. Fighting bravely, but with their escape routes blocked, the rebels were overwhelmed and annihilated. Tacitus later recorded that during the battle the Legate's son, Marcus Ostorius, earned the distinction of saving a citizen's life. We can only speculate that Antedios, too, was also involved in the scrap.

The Iceni background at this point is still very clouded, but it looks as though the local political scene was riddled with bickering and infighting between pro- and anti-Roman groups, and perhaps even between the various tribal centres, possibly Caistor, Warham and Threxton. Another possibility is that the troubles were confined to the western sector and that Prasutagus, ruler in the east, eventually took over.

Near Woodcock Hall (Robin Brown) it is likely the Romans razed the Iceni settlement as part of the punishment, and then built a small fort still large enough to hold 480 men, part infantry and part cavalry. If disaffected tribesmen did indeed remain in the area for a year or two after AD47/48, then this military mix would have been ideal for dealing with them - the Gaulish cavalry, who would have known the local language, ranging far and wide, the infantry guarding the crossing of The Straits stream and possibly (see Chapter 3) keeping an eye on the Peddars Way.

Strange to relate, within a surprisingly short time the Iceni were being given special privileges by the Romans, further evidence, perhaps, that only some of the tribe had stepped out of line and that the rest, by and large, were ready to resume the relationship. Anyway, the rift was apparently patched up even though Scapula may have insisted on a change of leadership. It is possible this was how Prasutagus came to the fore, as head of a new federation of pro-Roman Iceni tribes.

In fact the argument seems to have been more than merely patched up. A substantial level of agreement was reached. The Iceni were given client kingdom status - in AD49, perhaps - with their own ruler, probably Prasutagus. It made them accountable to Rome and possibly, technically, outside the governing sphere of the province. In effect, they seem to have been given token independence, allowed to keep their trappings of the past and to live in token freedom on the edge of the empire. The king knew he was ruled by the emperor and that he was expected to name the emperor as his heir; on the other hand the Iceni, provided they paid tribute and accepted aid in the form of loans, were presumably allowed to keep their weapons, their chariots, their coinage and some of their laws and institutions.

There were advantages to both sides. The military men of Rome did not have sufficient numbers of troops available to pin down the entire region and pursue campaigns elsewhere. This deal secured East Anglia without using any front line troops. It also recognised the geographical importance of the Icenian territories which were relatively close to Colchester and which, perhaps just as importantly, also controlled sea routes on the east coast of the Wash and the Norfolk estuaries. Indeed, perhaps the agreement included some sort of Iceni guarantee of protection for Roman supply vessels and corridors of communication (see Chapter 3).

As for Marcus Ostorius Scapula, he was awarded the Corona Civica in AD48 to mark his gallant action against the Iceni rebels; but alas, he later committed suicide after allegations of plotting against Nero. As for Prasutagus, a somewhat remote and little known king, and possibly a Roman puppet, or compromise choice, he must have believed he had done his best for his people. On one coin he is depicted as young, long-nosed and wide-eyed, and with a full head of wavy hair. This may have been a public relations job, of course. But at least he had seized his moment and for a decade he was able to lead a comfortable, even wealthy existence with his kingdom at peace. And he had his family around him.

Meanwhile, the military campaign in the west rumbled on, finally bringing southern England, the Midlands and Wales under Roman rule. The one exception was the island of Anglesey (Mona), which gradually became a final rallying point for the Druids, the intellectual leaders of the tribes, and a haven for the last of the warriors who still opposed Rome.

In AD54 Claudius died in somewhat suspicious circumstances leaving the way clear for his stepson, Nero, to ascend the throne. For a time it seems Nero contemplated bringing the troops home and abandoning completely the conquest of a troublesome Britain, but he seems to have decided to keep the good name of Claudius unblemished. And so in AD58 or 59, by which time the governor was the tough and battle-hardened Suetonius Paulinus, the order was given yet again to finish the job and move against Anglesey and the Druids. It was a pivotal point in the story.

The history of our first national heroine is clouded by many things, including doubts over the spelling of her name. Tacitus, translators would have us believe, called her Boudicca; the Tudors and Stuarts knew her as Voadica, or even Bonduca; and the Victorians as Boadicea. Current thinking seems to lean towards Boudica - pronounced Boo-dikka - meaning Victoria, Victory, or the Victorious One. The Celtic word for victory was bouda and modern Welsh, so I believe, embraces the word buddug. Another thought is that her name may not have been personal, but a hereditary religious title for the female line. But these are small, academic matters. The real starting point in attempting to clothe the bones of the story was AD59 or 60, when she was described as "royal," as the widow of Prasutagus, and as the mother of two daughters who had presumably, though not necessarily, reached the age of puberty. There was no mention of sons.

Other Roman recollections describe her as having a commanding voice and long, red hair, and a liking for multicoloured tunics (kilt-like, presumably, or cloth dipped in vats of dye) fastened by a brooch and with a golden torc (a Snettisham model, a symbol of authority, perhaps) around her neck. She was also described as tall, which as John Peddie has pointed out may mean only 5ft 6in or so, for he recorded a study of Roman Britain skeletons which concluded that the average height of the male was nearly 5ft 7in, and the female, 5ft 2in. The rest of the picture is conjecture, but it has to be said that what comes to mind is of a mature, dominating and self-confident woman.

Peddie also recorded that the average life expectancy of the female, admittedly shortly after this period, may have been under 28 years (and just under 35 for the male), in which case it is possible Boudica was born somewhere around AD30 and her daughters around AD45-47, or just before the first Iceni revolt. By today's standards this would define her as a child bride; on the other hand, her daughters need not necessarily have reached the age of puberty at the time of the rape incident. But queries about her age aside, two other questions also spring to mind. Who was she, and where did she come from?

One easy scenario is that she came from a pro-Roman faction, perhaps from within the Iceni or from another tribe, possibly the Trinovantes, the Coritani or even the Brigantes of the north. It is interesting to recall that the Brigantes were also led by a woman, Cartimandua (her name meant Sleek Pony, apparently), the lady who finally got her hands on the defeated Caractacus and handed him over in chains to the Romans. Another scenario sees the marriage of the two, Prasutagus and Boudica, bringing together, politically speaking, the dispersed focal points of the Iceni, the Brecklands (or West Norfolk) and Caistor St Edmund. Whatever the truth, circumstances point to an aristocratic though not necessarily royal background.

In addition to a woman of considerable maturity, what also comes to mind is someone accustomed to wielding authority. This was not unusual among the Iron Age tribes. Women are known to have been powerful figures, socially, physically and politically. Indeed Tacitus, in trying to make us believe he had a verbatim copy of Boudica's AD60 pre-battle speech, but in what reads as something much closer to a Roman comment on the situation, quoted her as saying: "We British are used to woman commanders in war."

She would certainly have been versed in current events. Even if her childhood had been spent in a country free from Roman domination, if not from Roman influence, she would have known of Roman traders and goods; later, as the wife of Prasutagus, she would have had a grounding in the politics and machinations of Cartimandua, Caractacus and Togodumnus, and the fearful Catuvellauni.

There seems to have been another side to her as well, for there was also a religious dimension to the revolt of AD60. Again, Tacitus, in recording her pre-battle speech, also has her saying: "I am fighting as an ordinary person, for my lost freedom, my bruised body and my outraged daughters. The gods will give us the vengeance we deserve." It was also reported she prayed to the god Andraste, though experts have not been able to nail this one. The closest they can come up with is Anu, the Celtic "mother of mothers," Andarte, a goddess of south-east Gaul, and more significantly perhaps, Andate/Andrasta, evidently a British goddess whose name also means Victory (that word again!), or invincible.

Of course, it is easy to suggest a substantial Druidic influence but less easy to pin-point it. Nevertheless, the Druids must have been a factor. They were the intellectual base of Celtic society as well as an important religious and political influence. Evidently free to cross tribal boundaries they were also the learned class of their day. They seem to have been responsible for the gold trade, too, and may have had connections with the Iceni and the sea ports around the Wash and the North Norfolk coast. Operating out of sanctuaries, Anglesey being the last to survive, one of their ceremonies may have involved the ritual filling of wells, two of which have been found in Norfolk.

Peter Berresford Ellis gives them an additional gloss, arguing that they were given a bad press by the Romans, who made blatant efforts to suppress them, and romanticised out of all recognition by 17th and 18th century antiquarians. He suggests there is a possible parallel between the Druids and the Brahmin of the Hindu culture, pointing out that whereas Druids could sometimes be kings not all kings were Druids. They were spiritual, they believed in collective ownership and they included women in political and religious life, all of which would have been anathema to Rome's rulers who would certainly have seen them as a threat to the order of things. No doubt Boudica was at least familiar with their ways, though as Berresford Ellis writes, tribal acceptance of her as a war leader suggests an argument could be made out that she "was a Druidess as well as a queen," and possibly a priestess of Andrasta.

The attack on Anglesey, masterminded by Suetonius Paulinus, and the bitter fighting and atrocities that followed warrants little place in this account save for the fact that at the moment Roman victory was secured a messenger arrived bringing the commander news of a serious uprising in the largely unpoliced Iceni territory. Suetonius knew he had to act quickly. He had with him the complete 14th Legion Gemina from a base in the Midlands, perhaps Mancetter (Manduessedum), elements of the 9th Hispana, based at Longthorpe, near

Peterborough, and detachments of the 20th Legion Valeria from Gloucester (Glenvum), plus auxiliary regiments. All told, about 20,000 troops.

But having stripped garrisons and sentry posts his military lines were stretched and the bulk of the troops positioned far away from this new and disturbing flashpoint. He realised that if numbers of tribes joined the uprising then he risked losing the province. One irony in particular must have riled the Roman command. The trouble had been started by a woman.

The reasons behind the uprising of AD60 are likely to have been numerous. They are certainly not clear, though pressures do seem to have been building up for some time. Dear old Prasutagus, moderate, wealthy and astute to the end, had died, perhaps circa AD59, whereupon it was found that he had attempted in his will to keep some of the old ways intact by dividing his property and lands between Nero and his family. Perhaps he wanted his daughters to take Roman husbands. Whatever the precise reading it infuriated Nero and his cronies. The realm and the household were plundered, Boudica is said to have been flogged and her daughters raped. Iceni chiefs were stripped of their ancestral lands and the king's relations treated like slaves. Indeed, Tacitus suggested the revolt was sparked by the "woes of slavery" and by "violence and insult" from the legates and procurators who wreaked fury on Iceni lives and property.

There were also hints of financial chicanery involving Nero's financial agent, a certain Catus Decianus, who seized the opportunity to demand repayment of loans authorised by Claudius. Many of the debtors had turned to money-lenders, one of them being Seneca, who evidently lent vast sums at high rates of interest. Presumably this cash was used to pay off Catus Decianus, who in turn paid Nero. Then Seneca called in his loans. In any event the selling of property and livestock, and widespread ruination, seems to have been the outcome. One assumes that Suetonius, the professional soldier who had a major campaign on his hands on the other side of the country, took little part in this or at least did not intervene. Certainly it was a blundering episode totally mishandled by Roman civil servants who failed to grasp how delicately the province was balanced.

All in all it was a complex and ghastly business, and one still not fully understood. So perhaps the revolt was sparked by a whole package of grievances - the beatings and rapes; greed; fears that Nero would snatch the best lands and effectively reduce the kingdom to occupied, provincial status; resentment that such treatment should have been handed out to a largely pro-Roman people; anger over wealth draining away to money-lenders; news from Gaul that the Romans were not militarily invincible, after all; and Druidic promptings emphasising, no doubt, that here was a timely and perhaps final opportunity to rid the country of the invaders. After all, if Boudica was a sacred leader, then the hurt against her and her family was plain and simple blasphemy. Perhaps, too, the Iceni found eager allies in the Trinovantes, keen to win back their capital, and in a new generation of Catuvellauni warriors eager to avenge defeat and rid themselves of burdensome taxation. Anne Ross (A Travellers' Guide to Royal Roads. Historical Times Inc & RKP, 1985) also suggests that the Coritani (Leicestershire), Cornovii (Shropshire), Dobunni (Gloucestershire), Durotriges (Dorset) and the northern Brigante may also have joined in.

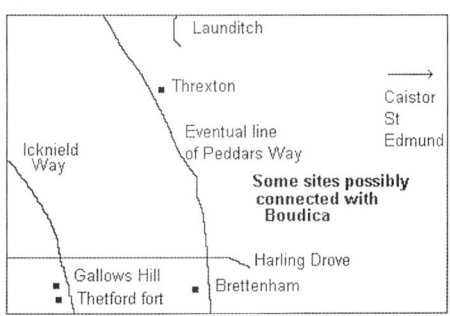

Whatever the cause or the theory it was time for Boudica to step out from the shadows. Tacitus said "the whole island" now rose under Boudica, "a lady of royal descent - for Britons make no distinction of sex in their leaders." The implication is that tribal crisis meetings were held. Dio recorded that when Boudica had finished speaking "she consulted with the will of the gods by letting a hare escape from the folds of her robes. It ran in what they considered to be a lucky direction, and the crowd gave a mighty cheer." Then she raised her hands and said, "I thank you, Andrasta, and call upon you as a woman speaking to woman ... I beg you for victory and preservation of liberty ... Mistress, be forever our leader."

It is interesting to ponder where these gatherings might have taken place and disappointing that archaeology has not so far been able to supply answers. Perhaps it was at the ceremonial centre at Fison Way, just outside Thetford. At Threxton. Or at Caistor, perhaps. And what time of year was it? It may have been in the spring. If so, were the crops already planted or were fields simply abandoned? Certainly subsequent famine was high on the probability list. But all that aside somewhere in Norfolk, or on the Suffolk border, a huge, anarchic mass of angry people came together. Armed peasants, warriors, charioteers, stores wagons, horses, wives and children, a shambling, excited, chaotic crowd which, given the word to move, finally began to hunt down the small groups of Roman troops in their scattered outposts. The way to Camulodunum opened before them. Roman Britain teetered on the brink of collapse.

Colchester (Camulodunum) had been a focal point of discontent for a long time. In about AD49 the old tribal centre had been turned into a Roman veterans' colony, Trinovante lands seized and the Britons treated as second class citizens. To rub salt into the wounds a huge temple dedicated to the "divine Claudius" was founded probably after AD54, which locals must have seen as an emblem of subjugation. More to the point the settlement had few troops, aside from some retired military veterans, and no prepared defences.

When news of the slowly advancing horde reached the town the streets seethed with rumour. Panic set in and the bewildered elders prevaricated. There was no evacuation and evidently no attempt to organise defences, but they do seem to have sent word to Catus Decianus in London (Londinium) who, in a largely unsympathetic and apparently half-hearted gesture, eventually sent nearly 200 poorly armed men to bolster the utterly outnumbered residents.

Boudica's rebels surged on. Then, before they reached Colchester, there occurred one of those incidents which add greatly to the fascination of the story. Someone, perhaps a soldier or messenger from a military outpost, galloped post haste to the nearest base with news of the uprising. John West (Roman Lincoln. Watkins, 1991) said the message was sent to Lincoln (Lindum), while other writers claim the news was received at the headquarters of the 9th Legion at Longthorpe, near Peterborough. Which ever base it was, it was many miles away, representing hours of hard riding. As it happened most of the 9th were away supporting the attack on Anglesey, but the man in command of the remainder, Petillius Cerialis, took a brave and immediate decision to try to intercept the rebels, or at least slow their advance. He managed to gather a detachment of about 2000 men, including a small detachment of cavalry, and hurried south-east.

Militarily it was probably the correct thing to do, but it proved a monumental disaster. Perhaps Boudica had an efficient intelligence network. Anyway, somewhere on the march the Romans were caught in an ambush. Tribal charioteers may have come across them in open country. The Roman infantry was massacred and Petillius Cerialis and the remnants of his column had little alternative but to turn and hasten back to base. At Longthorpe, at least, signs of a small, temporary defensive position hurriedly built inside the main fort lend weight to the possibility that some of Boudica's elated followers may have whooped after them in hot pursuit.

Longthorpe did at least manage to get a message off to Suetonius, but Colchester was doomed. The horde fell on the settlement with a frenzied hatred. Those residents who had taken to arms fell back to the only available solid structure, the temple, and they managed to hold out for a time. Eventually, of course, they were overwhelmed. Dio Cassius says the British rounded up captives for slaughter in the sacred grove of Andate, or Andrasta. No-one was spared and the destruction was widespread.

Boudica's victorious rebels seem to have remained in the area for some time. Perhaps she was not certain what to do next. Or she may have been awaiting the arrival of tribal reinforcements from elsewhere in the country. Her options included an attack on St Albans (Verulamium), in Catuvellauni territory - another opportunity to settle old scores - or London, then a haphazard and undefended trading post thronged with merchants which clung to the riverside surrounded by marshy river flood plains, open country and thick woodland. Just as importantly for Boudica, it was also the seat of the hated Catus Decianus.

She must have known the 2nd Legion Augusta was stationed at Exeter (Isca) and that sooner or later Suetonius would break off his campaign in Wales. Thus it may have been for military reasons, or even a burning desire to catch Catus Decianus, that she chose to attack London. If the 2nd was perchance confronted and defeated virtually all of south-east England would have been liberated; but Exeter was many days march away, which would have given Suetonius ample time to regroup. London still stood in the way, and with luck she might even lure Suetonius into a futile defensive action.

As the horde rested in Colchester after its excesses Suetonius acted with speed. He decided to gallop to London to assess the situation for himself, and ordered the bulk of his army to follow as quickly as possible. He also sent word to Poenius Posthumus, commander of the 2nd, ordering him to set his troops on the march and presumably meet the main force somewhere.

It would have been an awesome sight. Given time for preparation each soldier was accompanied by 17 days' rations, some of the load being carried by pack animals. For an army on the move, therefore, it would have meant transporting tons of grain and fodder, a long supply train, and carts and wagons carrying arms, armour, artillery and water.

Indeed, John Peddie (The Roman War Machine. Alan Sutton, 1994) calculated that, in addition to base and supply camps, an army comprising six legions, including cavalry, staff officers, supplies, baggage and services, would have needed some 7500 horses or mules and that the baggage element of such a column might have extended nearly 13 miles. For the rest, no doubt they foraged and thieved as they travelled. Suetonius, though, may have ordered his troops to travel light and as quickly as they could.

Anglesey to London is about 260 miles, and even with relays of fast horses it would have taken Suetonius several days; but once there, it would have taken him only a short time to realise the settlement was doomed. There were no defences, the 2nd had not responded or in any event did not respond, the reserves from the 9th had been massacred, the main body of his army was still many days' march away, and he may have been short of supplies. He decided to withdraw and leave London to its fate.

It was a difficult but necessary decision, and one may imagine him surrounded by a throng of pleading worthies, merchants and administrators frantic with worry. After all, the post was probably stuffed with merchandise and plunderable goods. But the level-headed Suetonius turned away and headed back the way he had come, "taking those who would follow as part of his column" (Tacitus). We are left to wonder if it was a strategic withdrawal or if he was actually being chased.

It is not known why Poenius Posthumus and the 2nd failed to respond to orders. Tacitus said he merely locked the gates of the fort at Exeter and waited until the rumpus was all over, but it seems unlikely that cowardice was the reason. Posthumus was a military man. With the country in uproar perhaps he judged it a bad time to attempt such a march. Maybe the tribes of the south-west were also in uproar and that there was a very real threat to the fort. We may never know. History merely states he did not do as he was told.

Boudica's army and followers, meanwhile, moved again. There is some evidence (Essex Archaeology, No 4, reprinted in the Essex Chronicle, September, 1987) that Chelmsford (Caesaromagnus), on the line of the main Colchester to London road, may also have been attacked, for an excavation at Godfrey's Yard hinted at the town's origins as a military and official post beside the road and uncovered a temporary military earthwork. Yea or nay, it cannot have delayed Boudica for very long.

On they swept, presumably, over the heights of what is now Billericay and South Weald and the tangled estuaries of the rivers Roding and Lea and the damp plains of Wanstead, Leyton, Clapton and Old Ford, finally swooping on the terrified community. To the south and west, no doubt, river bridges and roads were packed with fleeing, frightened refugees. They were right to hurry away, for the latest orgy of bloodletting and slaughter seems to have been uncontrolled and full of religious and patriotic frenzy. It left London in flames.

In time, Boudica marshalled her followers, by now sated with blood and plunder, and led them to St Albans (Verulamium), the old Catuvellauni centre, on which they must have fallen with particular relish.

Years later Tacitus was to claim that 70,000 Roman citizens died in the three centres. Whatever the figure, there is no doubt the cost in human terms was high. But what is bloodthirsty? Berresford Ellis relates that Trajan (AD98-117) could put 5000 pairs of gladiators into the arena and force them to fight to the death, and that tens of thousands of "criminals" were ritually slaughtered. Only when Rome was invaded by people the Romans called "barbarians" did the bloody spectacles come to an end.

Boudica must have sensed that Roman fortunes were at their lowest ebb. Equally, it could be argued that Suetonius was beginning to take control of the situation and even dictating events. Certainly he would soon be reunited with his main force and he was luring the rebels ever closer to a set-piece battle. With Boudica's followers preoccupied, Suetonius, possibly being harassed by the tribes, awaiting reinforcements, and most likely short of food - amid the hard marching there would have been little time for scavenging - could at least dictate the site of the battle if not the actual moment.

He evidently chose well, picking a place near Mancetter (Manduessedum), Warwickshire, which Michael Wood (In Search of the Dark Ages. BBC, 1981) relates to "the place of chariots." Here his rear was well protected by thick woodlands while the rebels would have to attack uphill and over a stream. When the main army arrived he ordered the weary troops into battle readiness. Then he waited. By now it must have been late in the year, perhaps autumn.

Some reports claimed that 10,000 professional Roman troops ultimately faced 250,000 undisciplined rebels. Again, reports also claimed that 80,000 rebels lost their lives against 400 Roman deaths. Make of the figures what you will. They all come from the Roman side. What did seem to happen, however, was that the rebel chariots proved useless on the saturated ground, that their ranks broke under the weight of disciplined attacks by javelin and sword, and that the Britons were forced back against the barricade of their own wagons.

Boudica's ability to rally, organise and inspire finally deserted her, and warriors, women, children and animals were slaughtered. The professionalism and organisation of the outnumbered troops triumphed. "It was a glorious victory," Tacitus commented later. The Roman province was safe for 350 years, but the Iceni tribe died that day.

Suetonius seems to have decided upon a wide-ranging and salutary revenge. Those survivors who did manage to leave the battlefield presumably scattered or tried to make their way back to the homelands. No doubt they were pursued and, if caught, dealt with on the spot. All the pent up emotions of the Romans, channelled into disciplined determination on the battlefield, now spilled over and the army, or at least the 9th Legion, hacked and harried its way back to the Iceni heartland. Suspects were rounded up, homes plundered and burned, and the structure of tribal life systematically dismantled and destroyed.

The task, apparently pursued with unusual viciousness and thoroughness, spilled over into the following year, for it is known the army spent the winter in regulation-issue leather tents. Crops were unsown, fields and herds untended. Manpower was short. Essentially, the tribal economy was shattered. Norfolk burned and the population was decimated, and starvation hovered over the ravaged land.

No archaeological site in Norfolk has yet produced any evidence of this period of Roman revenge, but it is assumed many settlements were abandoned. Only the vast and enigmatic Gallows Hill/Fison Way site near Thetford gives a hint of what might have happened. Laboriously developed and expanded during the 20 years or so before the rebellion, its usefulness was abruptly ended. Hundreds of timbers were removed, either by the military, who may have fretted over its defensive potential, or by a military-controlled labour force. Perhaps the military commanders needed the timber to build fortifications elsewhere. There was certainly plenty of it - the encircling artificial grove comprised a nine-deep complex of massive fences, possibly associated with Faunus, a woodland deity. But there may have been more to it than this. The site also commanded clear views of the key Icknield Way corridor and the river crossing at present-day

Thetford. "I suppose it (Fison Way) might be described as the gateway to Norfolk," the late Tony Gregory once said to me.

Of course, the Romans were great users of timber. In 1994 it was reported that archaeological work not far from Hadrian's Wall had produced hints of dramatic changes to the landscape of Cumbria and Northumberland when the Roman army was stationed there in the 2nd century AD. There was evidence they had cleared vast tracts of woodland, not just to produce an obstacle-free zone, but for timber, and to clear land for crops and grazing flocks. In Carlisle a military turf and timber-built fort erected in AD72-73 was said to have consumed several million cubic feet of wood.

On the other hand, perhaps the destruction of Fison Way could be put down to sheer bloodymindedness. Dio Cassius commented that the shame of the rebellion, allied with the destruction of Colchester, London and St Albans, was all the greater because it had been engineered by a woman. We can only guess.

And the aftermath? Well, the 14th Legion received the triumphant title of Martia Victrix along with an envied reputation for invincibility, while the men of the 20th earned the right to be called Valeria Victrix. A few years later the 14th Gemina was withdrawn from Britain for duties elsewhere. More immediately, troop reinforcements were hurried in, the Fison Way site was dismantled and carted away and Caistor St Edmund (Venta Icenorum) ultimately became a small Roman town and local administrative centre. The site may have been chosen because of a desire by the Romans to break completely with the tribal past, or as a means of dominating a former tribal heartland with a regime of their own. On the other hand a small number of dedications to Neptune discovered there suggest the river Tas may have been navigable from the sea.

As for people we have already met, the shamed Poenius Posthumus, commander of the 2nd Legion who kept his men in their fort and thus denied them a chance of glory, committed suicide by falling on his sword; Catus Decianus, horrified by the scale of the catastrophe, fled to Gaul and was subsequently replaced as procurator by the peace-maker, Julius Classicianus, who reported to Rome that, really, Suetonius was the problem. As for Suetonius, he became the subject of a commission of inquiry - led by Polyclitus, a Greek ex-slave and civil servant - sparked by protests at the scale of retribution in the lands of the Iceni. He was quietly retired, an incident involving the loss of some ships being used as the lever to get him out. His replacement was the conciliator, Turpilianus.

Not many names, to be sure. Indeed, Antonia Fraser has pointed out that of the revolt, which may have involved over 100,000 people, only 10 real names are known, two Britons (Boudica and Prasutagus) and eight Romans. The only other known name distantly associated with the incident was that of Julia Pacata, widow of the fondly remembered Classicianus, who later commissioned a particularly fine tombstone for her dead husband.

As for Caistor, it has been closely studied but so far excavated only on a limited basis. And the key site at Threxton (Woodcock Hall)? Extensively fieldwalked and studied, but so far completely unexcavated. Could Threxton - close to Fison Way and even closer to the ritually-filled well at Ashill - have been the Camulodunum of the Iceni?

As for Boudica, she evidently survived the battle and fled the field. But where would or could she have gone? North to the Brigantes? Doubtful. Had Cartimandua chosen to throw in her lot with Boudica, and had her warriors joined the fray, Suetonius might not have survived. But Cartimandua seems to have remained loyal to Rome and the Romans may have retained a significant military presence in Brigantian territory. West, perhaps, towards Gloucestershire? A female skull discovered in a Celtic grave at Birdlip (which had East Anglian

The walls of Caistor St Edmund.

links largely through items of jewellery found in situ), and a subsequent cranium reconstruction, were displayed at Gloucester City Museum (EDP, June 29, 1995) labelled as "possibly" the face of Boudica. But why go west? Where could she have been trying to reach? Ireland, or Gaul? In any event, would there have been time for an elaborate grave construction and funeral? Other local stories link her final resting place with Garboldisham and Quidenham. But again, a time factor comes into play, and suggests otherwise.

Perhaps, more simply, Boudica merely tried to reach her tribal homeland in the Brecks, or even find a bolthole in the Fens in which case, from Mancetter, her route might have taken her by Market Harborough and Peterborough, or even Ely and Lakenheath. In any event she surely cannot have survived for long, and indeed, may have realised that her death might mean an end to the persecution of her tribe.

So with surrender unthinkable and Suetonius in pursuit, she died. Tacitus said she took poison, Dio that she became fatally ill. Perhaps both were right. No doubt she was buried by her companions, but where and when is not known despite many fanciful guesses. Dio Cassius wrote that when "Boudouica fell ill and died the Britons mourned her deeply and gave her a lavish funeral, and then they disbanded in the belief that now they really were defeated." My feeling is that, with the landscape burning and the smell of death in everyone's nostrils, her body was secretly laid to rest in a hurriedly dug grave in some forgotten grove. I like to think a Snettisham torc still lies with her. As for her daughters, nothing is known. The house of the Iceni had come to an end.

That Boudica came within an ace of changing the course of this country's history, and that she was the instigator of one of history's most remarkable incidents has been accepted for centuries. It must be said, too, that the aura of menace which enveloped the memory of her and her followers does still remain. The horrors of Colchester, London and St Albans cannot be forgotten. Perhaps these are modern feelings, though, and a modern reaction. In AD60 what had to be done was done. The Warrior Queen who set out to right great wrongs belongs to a different era. Now only her name, and the shadows, survive.

SELECTED REFERENCES AND READING

Berresford Ellis, John. The Druids. Constable, 1994.
Brown, Robin. The Claudian Fort at Woodcock Hall (article). The Quarterly, No 20. Norfolk Archaeological and Historical Research Group, 1995.
Chadburn, Amanda. The Iceni and their coins (article). The Quarterly, No 17. Norfolk Archaeological and Historical Research Group, 1995.
Davies, John. Iron Age Norfolk (article). The Quarterly, No 15. Norfolk Archaeological and Historical Research Group, 1994.
Fraser, Antonia. Boadicea's Chariot. Weidenfeld & Nicholson, 1988.
Grant, Sally. Boudicca. The Larks Press, 1995.
Ireland, S. Roman Britain, A Sourcebook (2nd edition). Routledge, 1996.
Kightly, Charles. Folk Heroes of Britain. Thames & Hudson, 1982.
Peddie, John. Invasion. Guild Publishing, 1987.
Robinson and Gregory. Celtic Fire and Roman Rule. Poppyland, 1987.
Royal Commission on Historical Monuments. London (Roman). HMSO, 1928.
Salway, Peter. The Oxford Illustrated History of Roman Britain. BCA, 1993.
Sims, Judy. Rebellion Against Rome (article). The Quarterly, No 19. Norfolk Archaeological and Historical Research Group, 1995.

Smallwood, John. De Civitate Icenorum (article). NARG News, No 20. Norfolk Archaeological Rescue Group, 1980.
Somerset Fry, Plantagenet. Boudicca. Allen, 1978.
Somerset Fry, Plantagenet. Rebellion Against Rome. Dalton, 1982.
Tacitus. The Annals of Imperial Rome. Penguin Classics, 1989.
Webster, Graham. Boudica. Batsford, 1978.

PLACES TO VISIT

So far Boudica has not been satisfactorily linked with any particular site or artefact. What follows is therefore somewhat conjectural.
Caistor St Edmund (Venta Icenorum). Post-Boudican town built by the Romans to dominate former Iron Age tribal territory. It is possible some of the early events leading to the revolt happened hereabouts.
Iron Age fort at Warham, near Wells, off the Wighton-Warham road. Again, no specific link with Boudica but lots of atmosphere to soak up.
Thetford Castle mound. Site of a former Iron Age fort which guarded the Icknield Way crossing of the river Thet.
Cockley Cley Iceni village and museum, between Hilborough and Swaffham.
Castle Museum, Norwich. There are displays on the Iron Age, Boudica, and the Romans.
Castle Museum, Colchester. Early history display covering the destruction of the city by Boudica, and a model of the Temple of Claudius.

At some point during the mid and late first century AD the Roman army of occupation in East Anglia built, or supervised the building of, a massive military road from Stanton Chare (Suffolk) to Holme on the North West Norfolk coast, a distance of over 50 miles. It became known as the Peddars Way, and much of it is now part of a network of local leisure footpaths. There have been a number of theories as to why such great effort was invested in the construction of a road which, today, seems to go nowhere, one theory being that a Roman ferry linked Holme with the Lincolnshire coast on the other side of the Wash. Thus the Peddars Way has often been explained away as the means by which 1st century AD travellers avoided a difficult journey across the Fens. However, the author wonders if the ferry theory really holds water.

3: Road *to* Nowhere

Allow me to declare an interest right at the start. The Peddars Way has been an interest of mine ever since a companion and I, new to the ways of walkers and burdened in our naivety by grossly inappropriate loads, took a week's holiday in a heatwave to stagger along the greater part of it. That was in 1973. Since then I have walked its Norfolk length numerous times and sections of it dozens of times; but this is largely irrelevant here. The fact of the matter is that walking got me interested in the Peddars Way, then in Norfolk's Roman roads in general and then, I suppose, in archaeology. It has been a diverting pastime ever since.

Thus it was with some hesitation I decided on this chapter heading (Road to Nowhere) because the Peddars Way has never been that to me. A means to an end, perhaps, and an intriguing puzzle, but never a dead end and certainly never a road without purpose.

Adding to the mystery and the fascination is the fact that in Norfolk there are other Roman "nowhere" roads, too, the so-called Holkham road, which seems to head towards the beach, and another brief length, from the deserted village of

Egmere to Barwick, which crosses the Holkham road at Haggard's Lodge. Both, according to Tom Williamson, "may have been like the Peddars Way, military creations, constructed to facilitate patrols and policing" after the Boudican revolt.

So far so good. Both the latter roads pass close to Iron Age forts (Holkham and Warham), though the latter may have been nothing more than a link with the Peddars Way; while the military derivation of the Peddars Way itself is not a matter of serious dispute. It is only when I come across casual references to the ferry theory that personal doubts arise. It has always seemed a too narrow and somewhat inadequate explanation.

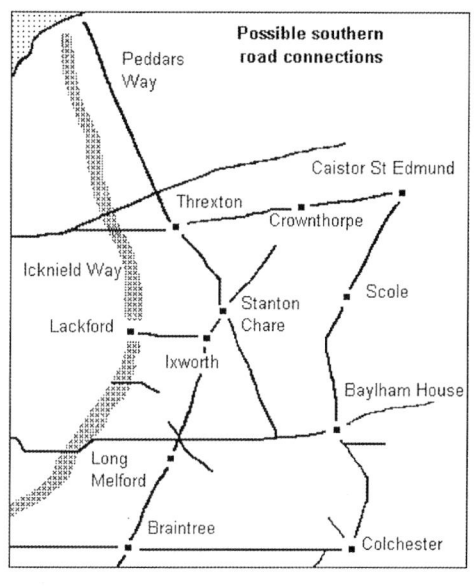

Of course, any attempt to fit the Peddars Way into the known pattern of Roman roads is still, of necessity, hedged with ifs and buts. In Norfolk, a small number of main roads seem to have formed the structural bones of what must have been a substantial network - the Peddars Way, from Stanton Chare or possibly Ixworth (both Suffolk) to Holme and the north-west Norfolk coast; the Fen Causeway, from March (Cambs) and Denver, with its eastern extensions, one branch of which took a northerly route through Fincham and Billingford to Brampton and beyond, and the other a more central route to Caistor St Edmund (Venta Icenorum) via Threxton and Crownthorpe; the so-called Pye Road, largely the modern A140, from Colchester (Camulodunum) through Scole to Caistor; and possibly Akeman Street, which may have continued north of Cambridge (Duroliponte) and on into Norfolk, skirting the fringes of the Fens.

It is generally assumed that the Peddars Way originally linked directly with Colchester, and indeed it would be somewhat surprising and decidedly odd if it did not. Indications of sections of a road from Ixworth seemingly leading south-east towards Colchester merely add weight to the conjecture.

The problem is that modern maps of the known network tend to imply a somewhat stronger link, at Stanton Chare and Ixworth, with another road from Chelmsford (Caesaromagus) and Long Melford which, at its north-east extremity, dies away in South Norfolk but may also have continued to Crownthorpe. So the junction at Stanton Chare would seem to be of prime relevance to the Peddars Way. By taking the left fork at Stanton Chare (Old English 'cerr' or 'cyrr' evidently meant 'turn') the traveller went to Holme; right, and most probably to Attleborough and Crownthorpe. Thus the oft-posed question: was the Peddars Way intended as a continuous route from Holme to Colchester, or was it restricted to the Holme-Stanton length, thereafter joining an apparently more minor route to Long Melford and Chelmsford?

Ivan Margary clearly saw the Peddars Way as a branch road even though it may have been more important than the source from which it sprang. Near Barningham Park, he wrote, the Way exhibited "a robust form of construction which is otherwise so notably absent from most of the East Anglian Roman roads. Apparently the Peddars Way . . . must not only have been constructed at a different date from the southern part of the road out of which it forks, but must also have been built upon more typically Roman principles and in weightier style." It was a point worth making, but it is possibly misleading.

Northern stretches of the Peddars Way do seem to have been more substantial constructions than those in the south-east, but recent writers have suggested this anomaly may be due to different soil conditions and therefore different construction methods. At Long Melford, for example, the Chelmsford road passes over sand and gravel, while the Bildeston (Colchester route) road was built on boulder clay. Nevertheless, the Suffolk roads were clearly important in their own right. At Rattlesden, one road was found to be 15ft wide with side ditches.

A direct link between Colchester, with its early military significance, and Holme, at the mouth of the Wash, seems the most obvious conclusion despite some south-eastern uncertainties still waiting to be resolved.

Nor has the route of the Norfolk stretch always been clear cut. In 1915 the archaeologist W G Clarke attempted to resolve some of the problems, pointing out that one infamous gap, between Threxton and North Pickenham, was plain to see on a map of 1797 (by which I presume he meant Faden's map of Norfolk). This particular missing link has therefore been missing for at least 200 years, and probably longer. There are other gaps, too, at Ringstead, for example, and yet another as the route approaches Castle Acre from Palgrave and Hungry Hill - possibly crossing or at least meeting the northerly extension of the Fen Causeway - to ford the river Nar.

This evidently strategic position (high ground, crossroads, river crossing) has produced surprisingly little evidence of Roman activity. Even the course of the road through the village is lost. There may have been a military post here, so perhaps much of interest still lies buried beneath the earthworks of the motte and bailey castle.

There are also minor uncertainties at Holme where, according to which diagram or map you look at, a fuzz of minor branch roads seems to meet up with the Way.

One ran to the much later shore fort at Brancaster (Branodunum) and another seems to have approached the beach at a slight angle to the main thrust of the Way. There may have been others. For example, C H Lewton-Brain (EDP. February 14, 1976) pointed out that Heacham once had an extensive salt panning industry, fed by the little Heacham River, but now alas obliterated. There was no suggestion the industry had Roman origins - though Domesday lists salt pans in the vicinity - but if it had, then perhaps there was a side road here, too. There were almost certainly numerous minor links between the Peddars Way and the Icknield Way.

In general terms the Icknield Way ambles leisurely along the lower western (seaward) slopes of Norfolk's chalk ridge, a fact which should not be seen as too surprising. Modern leisure walkers will confirm that the easiest route is often best. In any event, early users of the Icknield Way were hunters, not the hunted. The Peddars Way, however, seems to have run alongside the edge and to the west of the great swathe of lowland forest which once covered much of Norfolk's central boulder clay area. It also hugged the higher reaches of a ridge which surely provided a more conspicuous and direct route and which also allowed for a greater degree of watchfulness. Thus the road's speedier, higher and more prestigious line could also be construed as displaying a rather more guarded outlook.

There have also been a number of disputes over the Peddars Way, sometimes relating to obstructions and legal status, which in turn sparked flurries of correspondence in the EDP as to the road's origins, route and purpose.

One of the most famous eruptions was in 1930s when a fierce public debate was fuelled by the sudden erection of a number of gates and Trespassers Keep Out notices and the blocking of what had hitherto been stretches of public footpath. Thetford Rural District Council was called in to investigate and quickly discovered that the culprit was one of the area's newest employers, the Forestry Commission. In 1934, because of yet more problems over access and status, the highways (King's Lynn) committee of Norfolk County Council took on the task of surveying the entire length of the Roman road. They did it very thoroughly and more or less confirmed, from the evidence of ancient estate maps and documents, the route we accept and enjoy today.

The correspondence sparked by this publicity (EDP: December 6, 1930; February 7, 1934; October 12, 1978; and others) trotted out earlier arguments about pre-Roman origins (there appears to be no evidence one way or the other), different routes (some writers have claimed it went directly to Brancaster), Iceni war roads, and of course the ferry theory. A new entry in the field was a correspondent who suggested the Peddars Way was nothing more that a badger run.

There have been physical difficulties with the road, too, lack of use rendering some sections periodically impassable because of overgrown vegetation. W G Clarke said in 1915 that some sections were blocked by undergrowth; Eric Fowler (Jonathan Mardle of the EDP) reported similar problems in the 1950s; and I can vouch that a section near Anmer was difficult to navigate in 1973, brambles and nettles blocking the path. Since then things have improved, though there is still a delicate balance between the popularity of leisure walking, which can keep the road open for the whole of its length, agriculture, which tends to use sections of it, and nature, which continually wants to reclaim it.

Military origins

The case for a military origin for the Peddars Way rests on the size and substance of the road and the manner in which it seems to have been built, meaning its military specification and long, straight lengths, indicating speed of purpose and construction rather than a more meandering and leisurely approach. But as W G Clarke rightly pointed out, "No part seems absolutely straight; it winds more or less according to the nature of the country." The walker will confirm that this is so. If examined on foot, the ruler-straight route displayed on most maps is shown to be not wholly truthful. However, on the ground, and away from the very straight lengths, it tends to shift slightly rather than actually deviate. The only really obvious alteration in general direction, which also turns out to be little more than another gentle curve, is at Galley Hill (150ft), north of East Wretham (Stonebridge), where a little way to the south the Way crosses a small stream by a bridge once known as Stone Brig and where, according to W G Clarke, the court for the old Shropham Hundred was formerly held (see: The road in later life).

The construction of roads, at least in the early years of Roman domination, was a military task or responsibility, though local labour was almost certainly pressed into use. Indeed, individual gangs may have been responsible for particular lengths of the road, which may explain some of the unevenness of construction. Some military commanders may even have persuaded their troops that road-building was an honour, or a solumn duty, for S Ireland (Roman Britain. A Sourcebook. 2nd edition, Routledge, 1996) has referred to an inscription from Catterick dedicated to "the god who invented roads and pathways." It is not an entirely alien device. Medieval benefactors were sometimes convinced of religious mileage to be obtained in paying for the construction of bridges.

Roman roads were invariably surfaced with the best locally available material (in the case of Norfolk, gravel, flint, crushed stone, chalky clay), while brushwood or baulks of timber were sometimes used if marshy ground could not be avoided. Tellingly, I believe there are at least three places called Stone (or Stoney) Street at the southern (Suffolk) end of the Peddars Way route on the approach to

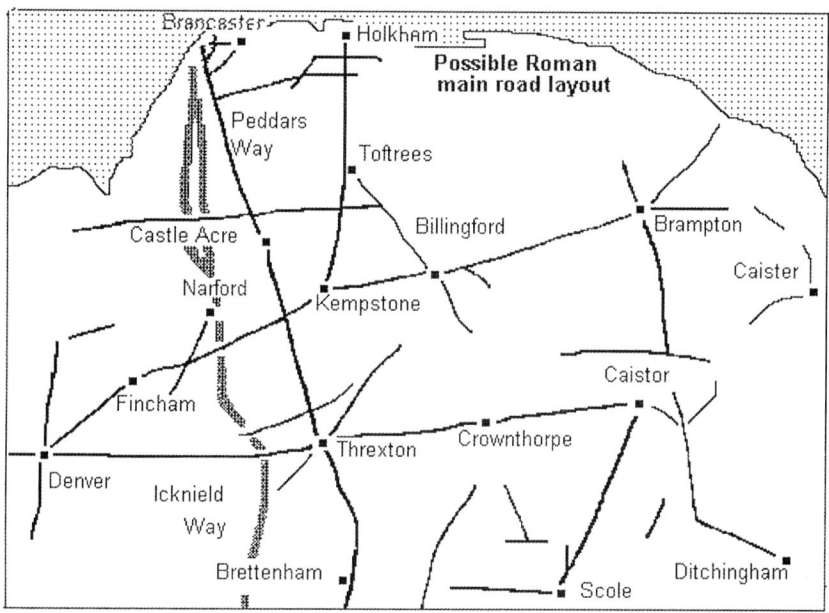

Colchester. The usual technique was to throw material dug from the drainage ditches on each side into the centre to form the agger (raised causeway: hence the nomenclature High Road, or High Street), while fords rather than costly timber bridges or pontoons were used if at all possible.

In Norfolk, the engineers faced a comparatively easy task. The county's section of the road rises gently from below 100ft, at the Little Ouse and Thet river crossings, to a mere 300ft or so at Shepherd's Bush, north of Castle Acre, before falling to sea level. The general line, as previously mentioned, is to the east of and slightly higher than the Icknield Way, though in the north-west of the county, closer to the shore, the routes move to within two miles of each other.

During construction, sightings for directional calculations were taken from the highest convenient ground, and the fact that Galley Hill marks the only real course adjustment in the whole of its 55 miles or so, and not a very major adjustment at that, is a remarkable tribute to the Roman military surveyors. They, of course, took the key decisions, designing a series of straight road sections with minor adjustments for ground conditions. These highly skilled professionals used, among other things, the groma (a form of sighting cross-staff) and the dioptra (for measuring angles and heights).

They seem to have run into problems at the crossing of the Little Ouse and possibly the Thet, two rivers now tightly confined by banks but which in Roman times presumably spilled haphazardly over wet and muddy floodplains. The Peddars Way (which crosses several watercourses en route from Knettishall to Holme) has a pronounced dog-leg at the Blackwater ford and another at Droveway ford, and a causeway on both sides of the Thet. There are also slight signs of an agger on Knettishall Heath. So it may be, given that both rivers still have soft, muddy bottoms, that the Z of the dog-leg was little more than an device to vary the places at which travellers crossed, to counteract over-use and erosion in any one area; or perhaps over the years there was some movement in the positioning of the best crossing places of the uncontrolled rivers.

Robin Brown, incidentally, has pointed out there may have been another dog-leg where the Peddars Way crossed The Straits, or the Watton brook, just south of Woodcock Hall (Saham Toney/Threxton). And at Castle Acre, particularly if Hungry Hill does indeed indicate the former line of the Way, then there is a clear indication of yet another Z-bend, this time over the Nar.

There have also been claims of stone fords at Droveway Ford (Thorpe Farm) and Blackwater Ford (Knettishall). An EDP correspondent (May 3, 1951) said that while working for the Great Ouse Catchment Board he was present when "a ford" was taken out of the river Thet. "The large flint stones were settled tight. Two Roman coins came out with the stones and silt. Down river about a quarter of a mile several pieces of broken unglazed pottery and horse or cattle leg bones were dredged out . . . I was told that another ford was taken out where the Peddars Way crossed the Little Ouse." All this is quite logical, though whether the stonework was of Roman origin is another matter.

As far as I am aware there is no hard evidence of a Roman bridge anywhere along the length of the road. However, there is a suggestion (again, Robin Brown) that baulks of timber were found at The Straits in the Watton stream bank near Woodcock Hall. These and other clues led him to conclude that the Peddars Way may have crossed the stream at this point and that there may have been a bridge.

How long did all this construction work take? It is impossible to say, though at least one attempt at calculation has been made. In the 1980s John Peddie put forward the idea of military "service" roads which were built quickly, making use of local materials, to support front line movements of operational troops. He asked the Royal School of Military Engineering at Chatham to study the time needed to build this sort of road - a cleared width of 8.6m with trees and scrub cut to ground level, a level carriageway of 2.6m marked by timber kerbs, and minimal or non-existent drainage. The calculations were based on the efforts of 1000 men working 10 hours a day.

Time taken varied greatly according to ground conditions (swamp, forest, heathland, grassland), but the engineers concluded that such a "service" road could have been built from Richborough to London (Westminster), a distance of about 120km, in about 15 weeks. On this basis a similar "service" road from Knettishall to Holme might have been completed in about 10 or 12 weeks. However, this is scarcely relevant to the final design of the Peddars Way, much of which was ditched, metalled and causewayed, and which was a far more substantial project presumably subject to heavier use. So what was the man-hours work/time ratio between a "service" road and full-blown military road? Did the latter take five times as long as the former? If so the Peddars Way, if it was a continuous rolling project, may have taken over a year to build.

Another factor is that some Roman roads appear to have been constructed across organised landscapes, the roads taking precedence over field boundaries, hedgerows and local lanes, sometimes (Muir & Muir. Hedgerows. Joseph, 1987) chopping established Iron Age farm fields into oddly-shaped fragments. Such treatment - which can still be seen today when a new bypass cuts a swathe through farm fields - is visible in the Tivetshall and Scole areas of South Norfolk, particularly relating to the so-called Pye Road. Here, pre-Roman fields were organised on a north-south alignment; the road, which took precedence, ran NNE-SSW.

Thus it is hard to believe that the laborious heavy construction work needed to build the Peddars Way could have been carried out in a violent or even sporadically hostile environment, even with a protective military screen. It would have pinned down hundreds of troops for months on end.

A measured response

On the Norfolk stretch of the road there are surviving lengths of agger (causeway) at Thorpe Farm and Brettenham, and at one or two other places. Slight mounds sometimes visible in the plantations near Galley Hill, which have been described as Roman, are more probably derived from Forestry Commission activities. One short section north of Harpley Dams, which has a worn and much-used surface, gives a slight impression of being raised up, or shelved, with a drop of several feet on the east side, but this may also be the result of agricultural operations. The sites of the roadside settlements at Brettenham and Threxton (and possibly even Castle Acre), seem determined by the position of rivers rather than by any official, regulation distance.

Raymond Chevallier says Augustus (27BC - AD14) decreed three road widths, according to status - 40ft, 20ft and 12ft. But such figures do not aid any attempt to formulate a Norfolk roads chronology. Wear and tear and modification have blurred the roadsides, and in any event, there is no certainty everyone measures from exactly the same place. I once measured 16 paces (about 45ft) from hedge to hedge on a stretch near Bircham, but again, this distance may have been distorted by parish boundary ridges, nearby farmland, and even by the hedges themselves.

Nevertheless such measurements, tenuous as they are, do demonstrate the road was not, in a constructional sense, a standard project but the result of localised amendments in terms of size and material. It is interesting that some stretches of it seem sufficiently wide to have allowed wheeled vehicles to pass each other.

Recorded width measurements, mainly for the Peddars Way, include - Barbara Green (EDP. January 11, 1965): At Brettenham the causeway was 16ft wide and 2ft 6in high, made of rammed flint topped with gravel. On the east side the rammed flint continued as a path at least 4ft wide. Another section north of the Brettenham and Bridgham road had an agger of rammed chalky boulder clay with a ditch on each side. Ivan Margary: Bridgham Heath, agger 36ft wide and 1ft high; Galley Hill, 36ft wide and 1ft to 2ft high; Harpley/Fring, agger 36ft wide and 1ft to 2ft high; near Fring, 45ft wide. W G Clarke: Fring, 20ft and 2ft high; Roudham Heath, dry ditch to the west, bank on east, 17 paces wide. "Width varies from 20ft to nearly 40ft." Norman Scarfe (The Suffolk Landscape. Hodder & Stoughton, 1975): Some roads (in Suffolk) little more than a bed of gravel 18in thick, there being no local stone. Widths (Baylham House to Scole road) include 21ft, 23ft and 32ft. Bildeston road (which joins the Peddars Way at Ixworth), 15ft wide but with a flint bed under gravel.

The reference by Barbara Green to an extension to the Way at Brettenham, in the form of a 4ft path running alongside the road, is interesting. It may have been some sort of layby for travellers waiting to splash across the ford, or a place to stop and squeeze out their socks (I can confirm that in 1975, at least, the beds of the fords at the Thet and the Little Ouse comprised little more than sucking, knee-deep black mud); a place where wagons awaited their turn to cross the ford; or possibly it was in some way connected with Brettenham (the village of Bretta, or perhaps more importantly, the Britons) roadside settlement, which eventually housed a substantial Romano-British community.

Indeed, this particular area beside the Peddars Way has produced many Roman coins and finds over the years, none stranger than that reported by W G Clarke who said in 1915 that "a few years ago," in a sand pocket in the side of a chalk pit, a human skeleton was discovered standing upright. And in 1907, on the line of the Peddars Way, one skeleton and two other skulls were evidently found together with an iron spear (spearhead?) and part of a sword or dagger. He suggested it might have been the burial place of a number of Roman soldiers. More recently, Norfolk Archaeology (Vol XL11, part 2, 1995) reported an excavation at Melford Meadows which uncovered more evidence of Romano-British settlement, including a late Roman cemetery of 22 inhumations, four of which were decapitation burials.

The naming game

Aside from when it was built, why, and how long it took, another mystery attached to the road is the origin of its name. Peddars Way is not a Roman nomenclature. If the conquerors did have a name for it, then it is lost. Nevertheless, the name Peddars Way is very old. C H Lewton-Brain found the name "Peddars Way" relating to the Roman road on a Flitcham map of 1580-80, a Snettisham map of the 16th century, and on a 17th century Sedgeford map, which called it Street Way alias Peddars Way.

Karl Inge Sandred, of Uppsala University, who has studied Scandinavian placenames in Norfolk, listed (in a booklet sent to the author, 1979): Peddersty, 1423; Pedderes lane, 1425; Pedderesty, 1423-1462; Pedderysty, 1450s; Pedderstey, 1512; and Pedderstie, 1561. In the 1970s, at Norfolk Record Office, he also unearthed a 16th century map on which it was named Stretegate. Mr Sandred pointed out that the word sty has the meaning "path or narrow way," and is probably derived from the Old English stig, meaning "path," or possibly the Old Scandinavian stigr, which has a similar meaning. On the other hand, in the 1970s he was of the opinion that Stretegate might have been the older name, as the Old English word "stroet" meant Roman road.

Still on the subject of the road's many names, White's Directory, 1845, said it was "now called Pedler's Way," though this could have been a local change or even a corruption. W G Clarke pointed out that in 1915 the "middle section" of the road was often called Pedlar's Way, while in the south (Hockham, Roudham, Brettenham and Bridgham) it was known as Ridgerow Road, Ridge Road or Ridgeway Road. Presumably these were also local inventions.

The Medieval English word pedder seems to have been a derivation of the word pedde, meaning pannier, or pedlar, one who carried goods. A ped was also a semi-circular wicker basket, or pannier, for strapping on to pack animals and in which to carry produce. Norwich market (Priestly, Ursula. The Great Market. Centre of East Anglian Studies, 1987) once had an area for ped sellers, who laid them on the dirt surface of the market place and sold fresh fruit and vegetables straight from the basket. Of passing interest is the fact that R W Ketton-Cremer (A Norfolk Gallery. Faber, 1947) wrote of a Toby Pedder, one-time chief constable of the Smithdon Hundred, who was arrested in 1651 for persistent non-payment of tithes at Holme. The surname and the vicinity have an intriguing resonance about them, but it was probably no more than a coincidence.

I have often wondered if there was any connection, however slight, between the Peddars Way and the legend of the Pedlar of Swaffham. The church of Swaffham, not so many miles from the Roman road, has some wonderful pedlar carvings. Of course, the actual legend of Swaffham's pedlar makes no mention of the road, but the proximity of the two - the pedlar carvings and the name of the road - is intriguing. Ben Ripper (Ribbons from a Pedlar's Pack. Ripper, 1979) pointed out there was a certain John Chapman who paid for the erection of Swaffham church's north aisle following a masonry collapse in 1454. Ripper wondered if he was a chapman (barter man) reduced to the role of a pedlar. At the very least, Swaffham's pedlar may have used the Peddars Way regularly on his professional travels, or even walked a stretch of it to begin his journey to London to seek his fortune.

However, the general position seems to be this. The Roman name, if the road was given one, is not known. Stretegate may be the earliest known English name, though this may refer only to a portion of it. During the late Medieval period it seems to have attracted the name Peddersty, with several variations evoking redolent memories of gypsies and livestock, pedlars and pilgrims and passing trade; while early in the 20th century, or possibly before, other local names were attached to sections of the road.

Two other points. The name Peddars Way seems to have been in use elsewhere in East Anglia,

even though it has survived most strongly on Norfolk's Roman road. Others I have found are: W G Clarke (In Breckland Wilds, 2nd edition, EP Publishing, 1974) - document of 1585 says that Icknield Way near Beachamwell was once known as "Le Pedderysty alias dicta Saltersty," which implies a salters' road (shades of Heacham's salt pans, I wonder?); Norman Scarfe (The Suffolk Landscape. Hodder & Stoughton, 1975) - early manuscript maps of Fornham and

Barnham suggest that a road which seems to have linked the Icknield Way with the main Peddars Way was also known as Peddars Way; and there was a Peddars Way across the southern edge of Christchurch Park, Suffolk; Norfolk Archaeology, Vol 38, Pt 1, 1981 - map of Lessingham, dated 1587, which names a road near the common and leading to the church as Pedders Weye; and Vol 34, Pt 1, 1984, map of Mousehold Heath, Norwich, dated 1589, which marks a footpath as Peddars Way, as does a map of 1718. The second point is that the name still survives in areas other than those around the Roman road. Beccles has a Peddars Lane, as does Fulmodeston, near Fakenham.

So the name Peddars Way is not Roman, is not exclusive, and probably meant little more than a road for walkers or people carrying goods or produce.

Turning briefly to an allied subject, a cursory examination of over 40 place-names on or in the vicinity of the Peddars Way, using the definitions of James Rye (A Popular Guide to Norfolk Place-Names. The Lark's Press, 1991) suggests three of them might be classified as Old Norse (Thorpe, Thompson, Holme) while the overwhelming majority are Old English. Of these latter names, 18 seem to relate to crops, plants, trees, land or water, and 14 to individuals or families.

The ferry theory

It is time to look at the ferry theory. It seems to emanate from the writings of C W Phillips who suggested that the Peddars Way had been laid out as an approach road to a Roman ferry across the Wash. The idea has held sway for a long time. For example, Eric Fowler (Jonathan Mardle, EDP, September 9, 1959) believed there might have been a ferry port now beneath the sands beyond the tide-mark at Holme, while Barbara Green (EDP, January 11, 1965) pointed out that "the nearest garrison, 9th Legion, was stationed at Lincoln. If trouble arose the quickest route from there to East Anglia was across the Wash."

There is a great deal in all this, but the reasoning is glued together very largely by the fact that across the Wash, on the opposite shore some 20 Roman miles away (and incidentally, a Roman mile equals 1480 metres), is another substantial and, in its latter stages, ruler-straight Roman road. The sea intervenes, of course, but on a map the two certainly give the impression of heading towards one another, even if at least one more course correction would have been necessary for this to actually happen.

This other Roman route is the Lincoln to Burgh le Marsh road which (according to Margary in 1973) retained sections of agger and in one place was 30ft wide. It is interesting to note, however, that John West (1991) merely classifies this suggested Roman road as "probable." He also indicates another "probable" Roman road branching roughly north-east from this route towards Ludford and

Marshchapel. Some writers (for example, Parker & Pye, The Fenland, David & Charles, 1976) believed the Burgh le Marsh road may have led to a shore fort, arguing that local references to Chesterland or Casterland, prior to 1422, possibly indicate a Roman settlement of some sort in the vicinity of Skegness. A K Astbury (The Black Fens. EP Publishing, 1973), a strong supporter of the ferry theory, speculated that both the Burgh le Marsh and the Peddars Way roads once continued into the Wash to sheltered harbours, near Outer Knock Bank and Middle Bank, leading off the central channel.

Settlement. Shore fort. Sheltered harbours. These are all very well, but they move the argument a long way from a ferry, an explanation I have always believed suspect. In essence, why a ferry? And why such a massive road? It has never struck me as logical, as the theory would have us believe, that anyone at Venta Icenorum (a later foundation, remember), Camulodunum, Caesaromagus or even Londinium, mindful of the soggy malevolence of the Fens, would still elect to traipse all the way to Holme to board a ferry, with the appalling difficulty of weather, tide and current that this implies, simply to reach Lincoln (Lindum) or even York (Eburacum). Bearing in mind that the Fen Causeway is thought to have been an early construction, then in most of these cases a Wash ferry would not even have been the shorter route.

Such a link only seems to make sense in two directions, first, for a garrison at Brancaster needing to reach the Lincolnshire coast in great haste, and second, and as Barbara Green has suggested, for the 9th Legion to move into north-west Norfolk. Yet there are problems even here. Brancaster shore fort and its garrisons were several hundred years removed from the Boudican Revolt and the presumed construction date of the Peddars Way, and any need for the 9th to move into Norfolk at speed may have diminished rapidly after, say, AD65-70.

The date of the building of the Peddars Way is crucial to the debate. Essentially, it is anyone's guess. In fact it is notoriously difficult, if not nigh on impossible, to be precise about the construction date of most ancient roads. Found coins and artefacts discovered in situ tend to be the best measure. But in truth there might never have been an actual start date: ie, a track comes into being over many decades, then a series of tracks grows into a route. The process might take centuries.

Another particular difficulty as far as Roman roads is concerned is that comparatively little excavation time has been spent on them. Nevertheless, some attempts to dating have been made. Two Roman roads in Suffolk, including the road to Caistor St Edmund, have been dated to about AD70. At Coddenham, where the Caistor road bisects one of two superimposed early military forts, the road itself was dated at AD70 even though its origins might have been earlier. This estimate agrees with that of Rainbird Clarke (East Anglia. Thames & Hudson, 1960). The Fen Causeway, from Water Newton (Durobrivae) to Denver, has been dated merely to the 1st century AD (East Anglian Archaeology. Fenland

The road near Fring.

Project, No 4, EAA 52, 1991), thought it "possibly Neronian" and that it might have been connected to the legionary base at Longthorpe. Like the Colchester to Caistor road, therefore, it may have been one of the area's "early" constructions.

As for the Peddars Way, Susanna Wade Martins (A History of Norfolk. Phillimore, 1984) places it in the AD70-100 bracket, adding that it "linked north Essex with the Wash and Lincolnshire." Again, as a major military through route, it may have been one of the first to be built in the area.

Not unexpectedly there is little preciseness in these exercises, and even with constructed Roman military roads archaeologists often have to rely on general context to give them an inkling of their background. In this matter at least Norfolk is fortunate, for there is some extra, slight assistance. Often these clues are little more than faint field or crop markings, but they are called early military forts.

In East Anglia these marching or temporary camps, connected with the period of occupation after AD43 and the campaigns of reprisal and stabilisation after the AD60 rebellion, are quite distinctive to experts and they have been identified at Ashill, Swanton Morley and Horstead, and strongly suspected at Threxton (near Woodcock Hall; though this is thought to have been a "fortlet" rather than a camp), where evidence of early military activity has been found. Displaying the distinctive "playing card" corners typical of Roman military installations, some of these camps, whether occupied for a few days or for many weeks, could have been large enough to house a legion (about 5000 men) on the march. In any event John Peddie (The Roman War Machine. Alan Sutton, 1994) makes it plain the marching camps were part of a technique "specifically designed for operations deep in hostile territory."

It is clear from the number of East Anglian military sites that there was a substantial presence in the area particularly after the Boudican revolt, and if the four Norfolk camps are contemporary then from a map, at least, it looks as if the Romans built a military screen, or iron curtain, to contain or possibly divide the Iceni. It is known, for example, that Suetonius kept his army in the field in tents throughout the winter following the rebellion, and it is also known that reinforcements - 2000 regulars from The Rhine and eight auxiliary infantry battalions and 1000 cavalry - were rushed across the Channel to bolster the depleted forces and add teeth to the policy of suppression. Sheppard Frere (Britannia, Pimlico, 1991) has suggested some of the auxiliaries were kept in winter quarters, possibly at Great Chesterford, and that forts, or camps, were built at Chelmsford, Coddenham and Ixworth, in additional to those in Norfolk.

There was, undoubtedly, great activity, including summary justice, destruction, misery and famine; and it must be said at this point that the Fen Causeway, the Peddars Way and the Caistor road, taken together with the known early forts, have the ominous look of an unbearably tight stranglehold around the territorial throats of the Iceni.

Where the slaughter took place is anyone's guess, but we can speculate that groups of Roman cavalry ranged far and wide throughout the territory while infantry colleagues guarded key points. It goes without saying, of course, that a main army group on the move must have been an awesome and, to Iceni eyes, terrifying sight. A legion marched three abreast, with mercenaries deployed forward and to the sides as scouts. Each man carried food for several days, a cooking pot and skillet, clothing, weapons and trenching tools. Behind them came the quartermasters and drivers with long columns of baggage wagons and carts, mules and horses, carrying tents and fodder, stores and tools, and the rearguard.

By about AD66, or shortly after, the war and the reprisals were over. The military roads and the marching camps had been built, the troops were being withdrawn, and the Roman battle for local hearts and minds was about to begin. Ahead, perhaps by AD80, were local government units run by worthies whose fathers may have fought in Boudica's army, and later still, Roman dress and fashion, language and customs, and Roman stability. If the Peddars Way was one of the first, if not the first, military roads to have been built in Norfolk, then its original purpose had already begun to fade.

Maritime connections

It is time to try to put the Peddars Way into sort sort of context. There seems little reason to doubt its early military origins or that it was built somewhere during the AD47-70 period. It is also possible to believe that along parts of the route Roman engineers made use of and incorporated sections of older, native trackways, as W G Clarke argued. Indeed, it would be extraordinary to think that such routes, Bronze Age or Iron Age, did not coincide in places. And it is certainly pertinent that whereas today the Peddars Way passes through nowhere of size apart from Castle Acre, and possibly Ringstead, in Roman times it would probably have been nearer the mark to suggest that, Castle Acre aside, the road certainly passed through at least two major tribal settlements, Brettenham and Threxton.

Of Brettenham, David Dymond (The Norfolk Landscape. Hodder & Stoughton, 1985) has said it is now "interpreted as a market town rather than an agricultural village." While of Threxton, John Smallwood wrote, "The discovery . . . of a rich hoard of enamelled harness fittings made around AD50 . . . together with the Belgic-style enclosure with its ritually filled shaft of similar date from Ashill, make it as logical to accept as to doubt that at (Threxton) we have, in the commercial sense at least, the Icenian equivalent of Camulodunum, in all probability with its origins lying deep in the Middle Iron Age."

This realisation, or rather, the importance of these two sites, lend credence to the busy and rapier-like line of the Peddars Way. This, surely, is not a road which hurried towards the coast simply because of a ferry across the Wash, but a big road which strode by or even through important Iceni centres at Brettenham and Threxton, with all the military implications that this carries, and which then hurried on with yet another purpose in mind.

One difficulty which arises from looking at a map of known Roman roads in Norfolk is that the picture it presents is grossly distorted. For example, such a map does not indicate why or in what order the roads were built. Nor does it even show all the roads, because many others no doubt remain undiscovered. Indeed, looking at a map of known Roman roads in Norfolk is like examining, and trying to make sense of, a modern map which for some reason covers the period from 1645 to 1995 and which shows a handful of drove roads, one or two sections of turnpike and the odd mile or two of carriageway, with a scattering of green lane footpaths and town bypasses thrown in for good measure. In short, making assumptions is a foolish pastime.

Nevertheless, two Roman roads in Norfolk, the Peddars Way and the Holkham road (and possibly a third, beyond Brampton and on towards the North East Norfolk coast, though this is only a "probable" at the moment), seem to have a distinctive look about them in that they apparently approached the coast directly and urgently despite unknown destinations. They leave no doubt that, coastline and sea level changes accepted, the coast is the destination they intended to reach. The Peddars Way and the Holkham road both lead to areas of flat, shelving beaches where vessels could have been driven ashore, though the Holkham road, it should be added, also seems determined to reach an Iron Age fort which may once have been lapped by the tides. As a side issue, in Norfolk there are noticeably few known Roman roads leading to the coastline between Weybourne and Overstrand, where landing conditions might be described as more difficult, though it has to be admitted that agricultural operations over the centuries may have obliterated some routes.

On a map, at least, the Holkham and Peddars Way roads - and possibly the Brampton coastal road - look unique. Indeed, a few minutes spent examining the Ordnance Survey's Historical map of Roman Britain adds weight to the view. A search of the entire country, via the OS map, reveals that remarkably few other Roman roads approach coastlines, where no obvious Roman site is known, with quite the same urgency.

Among other possible contenders are: Colchester to Mistley (Stour estuary), Colchester to St Osyth (near Clacton), Learchild (near Ainmouth) to Tweedmouth (near Berwick-upon-Tweed), and of course Lincoln to Burgh le Marsh, to which John West has added another, from Ludford towards Marshchapel. One leads to a sandy estuary, one to a sandy, shelving beach, one to a muddy estuary, and the other to flat sands. None possesses the character and strength of purpose of the Norfolk roads.

W G Clarke was convinced the Peddars Way reached some settlement or other north of Holme "where in Neolithic times the sea-marge was nearly 30 miles northward of the present, a big triangular area having been destroyed by erosion." In fact a continuation of the Way by even 30 Roman miles would have produced a termination near Mablethorpe.

Clearly, a large section of former coastline has been lost; but let us suppose, in the political and military turmoil and the realignment and final agreement which seems to have taken place in AD47, or just after, dominant pro-Rome factions of the Iceni were given, among a number of privileges, the responsibility for overseeing the safety and smooth operation of Roman supply routes, perhaps along the Icknield Way, from the Norfolk portion of the Wash coast. Many Roman supply vessels navigating the Wash, the Metaris Aest, must have made landfall on the Norfolk (and the Lincolnshire) coast.

It would have been an arrangement, and a trust, which was utterly shattered by the Boudican revolt. After AD60, therefore, the Roman military authorities would have had no option but to police the north-west Norfolk and Wash landing areas themselves and keep an eye on several Iceni settlements including Threxton and Brettenham, and possibly another in north-west Norfolk.

There is another way of looking at it. The question of the incomplete picture given by maps of known Roman roads has already been mentioned. Another problem is that we invariably look at them with north to the top and south to the bottom, and indeed, printed words assume that. However, and just as an experiment, turn a map of Norfolk's Roman roads on its head and look at it again, from the point of view of a sea captain, not a landlubber, and from the perspective of a ship's crew looking to unload and be off with the tide. The map begins to take on a different outlook. In short, the Holkham and Peddars Way roads - as do Burgh le Marsh and Marshchapel - now look like inland routes designed so that goods and supplies, important travellers and Imperial postbags which have arrived by sea could be shifted to all parts of the country as quickly as possible.

An army-navy link may seem surprising now, but the Roman Imperial navy came under the military umbrella and was seen as

Crossing the Heacham River.

an extension of the army. Aulus Plautius, for example, had under his command a squadron of ships, the Classis Britannica, created and based at Boulogne. John Wacher (Roman Britain. Dent, 1980) commented that in the circumstances it was not surprising to find "soldiers undertaking seafaring duties." Tacitus described some of the vessels as "of shallow draught, pointed bow and stern, and broad beamed to withstand heavy seas." And John Peddie (The Roman War Machine. Alan Sutton, 1994) went so far as to suggest that the 9th Legion Hispania, from Pannonia, and indeed Aulus Plautius himself, may have been selected for the AD43 invasion of Britain because of the specialist water craft knowledge they had gained on the Danube. It was the 9th, of course, which advanced along the line of the Thames to the Medway, and then north up the East Coast.

The matter was also put succintly by John Orna-Ornstein (article, British Archaeology. Council for British Archaeology, No 8, 1995), commenting on the vital role played by Rome's navy, who wrote, "A navy based on war fleets, intended solely for direct combat, evolved first into an organisation of multi-purpose military vessels and then into a number of river fleets, composed of small vessels intended almost exclusively for transport."

It seems reasonable to suppose that some garrisons and legions in the field, perhaps in East Anglia, the Midlands, Wales and the north, and particularly during the years of turmoil in the mid and late first century, received some of their supplies - reinforcements and grain, for example - from vessels anchored in or beached along the shores of the Wash and the north-west Norfolk coast rather than the more distant South Coast. The Iceni must have been well versed in matters of maritime trade. They and the generations before them must have witnessed many landings and departures. Indeed, if Iron Age gold was shipped from North West Norfolk, as some have supposed, then they may have been experts if not in actual seabourne activities then at least in trading and loading and in keeping goods on the move.

Given an Iceni jurisdiction over Norfolk's Wash coastline and its beaches, estuaries and ports, and perhaps a busy and flourishing haulage trade, then one can see the Peddars Way, which was clearly built for speedy travel and to expedite the passage of wheeled traffic, in a slightly different light to that given off by the bare theory of a ferry to Burgh le Marsh.

Some of Robin Brown's conclusions are interesting, too. As far as Woodcock Hall (Threxton) is concerned, he believes that following the AD47 revolt the Iceni settlement may have been razed; that a small fort and garrison may have been present on Sand Hills (overlooking the Watton stream, which was much wider then than today) for five or six years afterwards; that the fort overlooked the crossing of the stream (where there may have been a bridge) and the main line of communication (south to Colchester, north to the next military base at Castle Acre); and that between Woodcock Hall and Castle Acre there may have been a signalling station at Robin's Hood's Gardens, Panworth, and possibly another near Little Palgrave Hall.

One implication of this is that even if the Peddars Way had not actually been constructed at this time, then a line of communication of some sort was nevertheless open. This in turn, I believe, enables one to paraphrase matters thus:

1. The AD47/48 revolt represented a flowering of anti-Roman resentment expressed by some factions of the Iceni. Afterwards, and for the next few years, small military garrisons stood guard against wandering, disaffected groups who may have posed a threat to key points.

2. Pro-Roman elements, represented by Prasutagus and bolstered by Roman troops, held political sway between circa AD47 and AD59-60. Part of the deal may have been that Prasutagus was responsible for the policing of Rome's supply routes from the Wash and the north-west Norfolk coast.

3. During the phase of violent retribution immediately following Boudica's rebellion of AD60, a heavy military presence was maintained in the area to exact revenge, finally crush the Iceni military power, and to protect communications and supply links.

If this is so then the Peddars Way was a multi-purpose road dating possibly from AD47, or more likely from the AD60 to circa AD70 period, when the Roman/Iceni bond had split asunder, and which enabled them to police at least two important Iceni settlements and guard landing beaches and supply routes for as long as necessary.

The road in later life

As for the road in later life, the evidence is slight. Seven or eight years after the revolt the uncertainties of the Year of the Four Emperors (AD68) occupied Roman minds when rebellion broke out among the army legions in Spain, Gaul and Rome. Nero fled and eventually committed suicide, to be replaced in rapid succession by Galpa, supported by the Legions and murdered by the Praetorian Guard, Otho, who lasted three months before committing suicide, Vitellius, who was executed, and Vespasian. And while this was going on, as Judy Sim has written, "the legions in Britain were divided as to who to support, complaining about the weather and apparently fed up with nothing to do except build roads." It is clear, however, that the Peddars Way remained in use as a line of communication for many decades, though the actual level of activity is difficult to determine.

As far as the Romano British period is concerned Tony Gregory noted that, together with the Icknield Way, the two roads "had no positive effect in attracting settlement sites." Nevertheless, sites had developed at Threxton and Brettenham, where the Peddars Way crosses rivers; a line of seven villas was built in north-west Norfolk along the Icknield Way, rather than the Peddars Way, perhaps because of water sources; and Brancaster may have acted as an economic and social focus for the north-west of the area. It led Gregory to conclude, in the absence of a known major centre, that the roads network was utilised by, among others, pottery distributors, while a mixed economy may have led to an unusual degree of local self-sufficiency. In this context it would be interesting to know to what extent Narford exerted an influence.

The Peddars Way did have a long and influential role in helping to define later local administrative areas, for about 50 per cent of the road dictates parish boundaries. For example, the parishes of Fring, Bircham and Harpley have eastern boundaries aligned with those of Snettisham, Shernbourne, Dersingham, Anmer and Flitcham and Appleton on the other side of the track. Swaffham and Sporle with Palgrave also make use of the Roman road (the name of the Procession Lane stretch of the Peddars Way between North Pickenham and the A11 possibly relates to the beating of this particular boundary); and so on. Two tiny stone parish boundary markers survive to this day on the edges of the track between the crossing point of the Little Ouse river and the A1066. Some 20 years ago, while flattening a patch of bracken and undergrowth prior to erecting a lightweight tent for an overnight stay, I came across an ankle-high ridge which continued parallel with the line of the road for an unknown distance. This was under the hedgerow on the eastern edge of the track between Anmer and Bircham. It may have been the result of agricultural activities; or it may be a surviving remnant of a linear parish boundary marker.

On a larger scale, parts of the Wayland and South Greenhoe Hundreds abut the road, and a section of the Freebridge Hundred runs alongside it. Some 33 Norfolk Hundreds were listed in the Domesday Book (AD 1086), by which time they were clearly accepted as units of administration and taxation. Thus they may have evolved from old tribal or territorial units - some of the Hundred names could reflect ancient folk groups - or after the English re-conquest of the area from the Danes.

Later, a line of markets along or near to the route also sprang up, charter dates including: Saham Toney and Watton (1204), Hunstanton (1225), Merton (1227), Thornham (1245), Swaffham (1257), Little Massingham and Hockham (1272), Stanford (1283), Harpley (1302) and Fring (1372). There were also markets at Thetford and Castle Acre. And the Peddars Way was still a significant, though not necessarily busy, part of the landscape in mid-Norfolk in 1600, as maps of the time show (Yaxley, David. Survey of the Houghton Hall Estate by Joseph Hill, 1800. Norfolk Record Society, Vol L, 1984).

At least one short section of the road was also used by pilgrims, including Royalty, travelling backwards and forwards to Walsingham. According to Rev L W Whatmore (Highway to Walsingham. The Pilgrim Bureau, 1973) the Walsingham Way route from the south came through Ickburgh and Weeting to South Pickenham and then to North Pickenham, where there was a hermitage, over "Piknamwade," presumably the river crossing on or very close to the line of the Peddars Way. They then proceeded along the Peddars Way the mile or so to where another Roman road once forked north-east towards Little Dunham. This fork was close to the point where the present Peddars Way crosses the Swaffham to Holme Hale road at the southern end of Procession Lane. Another main pilgrim route, said Whatmore, was through West Acre and Flitcham, which presumably

Photo (origin unknown) of Peddars Way, probably taken in the 1920/30s and possibly near Thompson. Note central groove worn by horses.

crossed the Peddars Way somewhere on Massingham Heath north of Harpley Dams.

The general feeling is that over the centuries the road has been used by gypsies and travellers, horses and carts, farmers and villagers, shepherds and flocks, pedlars and chapmen, and smallholders with produce to sell. In short, it became and was used as a rural footpath or green lane which, like so many others, fell into decline until brought into use once more as a haven for recreational walkers, horse riders and cyclists.

A tiny snapshot of sections of the road between about 1913 and 1944 can be seen in the delightful pen and ink work of Frank Patterson (Britain's Counties, Norfolk. GM Design, 1993), who travelled by bicycle "like some latter day Cobbett," and many of whose sketches were published in Cycling magazine in the 1940s. Some of his pictures suggest that the road was then still well defined and used by horses (a central rut cut by hooves is sometimes visible) and wheeled transport, including cyclists. One of his pictures was of the Peddars Way "near Thompson," possibly in the 1920s, with open heathland on either side and not a conifer in sight. Another, dated 1931, of a stretch between Roudham and Thompson, has scribbled on the bottom: "A Norfolk road which is to be cleared, repaired and improved - alas!" It is not immediately clear which stretch this was, but it could have been the presently metalled section north of the Dog and Partridge pub at Stonebridge.

Patterson evidently wanted his Peddars Way to remain as an untouched quiet rural backwater. In that sense, feelings have not changed.

SELECTED REFERENCES AND READING

Barringer, J C. Faden's Map of Norfolk, 1797. Larks Press Edition, 1989.
Brown, Robin. Field walking at Woodcock Hall (article). Norfolk Archaeological Rescue Group News, No. 10, 1977.
Brown, Robin. The Claudian Fort at Woodcock Hall (article). The Quarterly, No 20. Norfolk Archaeological and Historical Research Group, 1995.
Chevallier, Raymond. Roman Roads. Batsford, 1989.
Clarke, W G. Peddar's Way (article). Proceedings, Vol 2, part 1. Prehistoric Society of East Anglia, 1915.
Frere, Sheppard. Britannia. Pimlico, 1991.
Gregory, Tony. Romano-British Settlement in West Norfolk and the Norfolk Fen Edge (monograph). BAR British Series, No 103, 1982.
Margary, I D. Roman Roads in Britain. Baker, 1973.
Moore, Ivan. The Archaeology of Suffolk. Suffolk County Council, 1988.
Ordnance Survey Historical Map and Guide, Roman Britain. Ordnance Survey, 1991.
Peddie, John. Invasion. Guild Publishing, 1987.
Robinson, Bruce. The Peddars Way and Norfolk Coast Path. Aurum Press, 1992.
Robinson and Rose. Roads and Tracks. Poppyland, 1983.
Salway, Peter. Roman Britain. BCA, 1993.
Sim, Judy. Rebellion against Rome (article). The Quarterly, No 19. Norfolk Archaeological and Historical Research Group, 1995.
Smallwood, John. De Civitate Icenorum (article). Norfolk Archaeological Rescue Group News, No. 20, 1980.
Wacher, John. Roman Britain. Dent, 1980.
West, John. Roman Lincoln. Watkins, 1991.
Williamson, Tom. The Origins of Norfolk. Manchester University Press, 1993.

PLACES TO VISIT

The Peddars Way is best viewed on foot, though it is possible to approach some sections by car.
In Norfolk, lengths of agger (causeway, or raised road) can be seen at Thorpe Farm (near Brettenham) or north of the river Thet.
Some of the best walking sections are: Knettishall (Suffolk) to Threxton; a short section (Procession Lane) south of the A47 near Swaffham; and Shepherd's Bush (near Castle Acre) to Fring Cross (near Sedgeford).

> At around midday on October 12, 1216, in the muddy vastness of the marshes and fens of West Norfolk and South Lincolnshire, there occurred one of those small historical events which somehow captured public imagination and later became enshrined in folklore. King John, ill and bad tempered, and hurrying north, lost his baggage train in the tide-wracked estuary of the Wellstream. He died a few days later at Newark. To this day argument and speculation over the incident continues, largely distilled into two questions: what, precisely, did King John lose, and just as importantly, exactly where did he lose it?

4: Lost *in the* Wash

To the hurrying traveller it is a local matter of minor importance, but to the native there is a subtle yet significant social difference between the black soil of the Fens and the brown furrows of marshland. I was born and bred in marshland amid the rich, chocolate-coloured clods of South Lincolnshire, and although we did not exactly look down on Fen folk, who grew celery, we of the cereal, potato and beet areas nevertheless felt ourselves worthy of the higher ground in most things, including geography.

As a youthful cyclist I was also breathlessly aware of the long, straight, raised causeway which stretched from the swing bridge at Sutton Bridge, alongside what was then the railway line to King's Lynn and the grass runways of RAF Sutton Bridge, to the very border of Norfolk, our promised land of beaches and hills and places to picnic amid the trees. To reach these sun-dappled delights we had to pedal across the causeway to Walpole Cross Keys before, so it seemed, properly beginning our ride to Sandringham or Hunstanton, or even Wroxham. It was always a battle. Breezes tended to congregate around the causeway and gather themselves into a mini-gale. You either puffed your way out of Lincolnshire, or back in.

And another, earlier, recollection. We were on the top deck of a Lincolnshire Road Car bus travelling to Lynn. Half way along the causeway, on the landward side, there came into view a pond, or pit, reedy-fringed, weedy and unloved, the water dappled by the wind. My father pointed to it, and said, "That is all that remains of the German Ocean."

He explained that the causeway spanned what was once a wide estuary, driven like a wedge between the two counties, and that once upon a time when there was no direct road travellers not wishing to undertake a long and tedious detour had to splash their way across the mud flats at low tide, mindful of the dangers and that within a few hours the sea would rush inland again as far as Wisbech. Even today the old road, now redundant, still seems to speak of some danger or other. Perhaps it is that vast unknown to the north-east, just beyond the horizon, the lurking sea, which is simply biding its time before rushing back to reclaim its own.

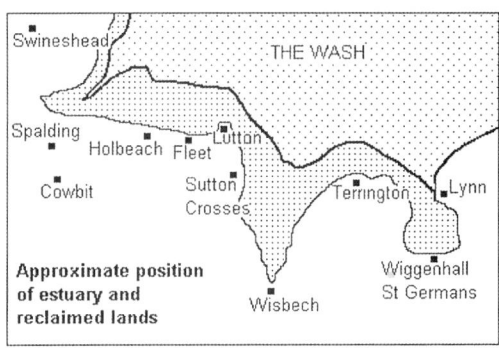

In 1969, some years after my father first pointed out all that remained of our bit of the German Ocean, he was one of the instigators of the restoration of a particular gravestone in Long Sutton churchyard. The inscription, which was re-cut, read: "This stone is erected as a memorial of Charles Wigglesworth, late of Sutton Bridge, coal merchant and guide for Sutton Wash 52 years, who departed this life, much respected, April 13, 1840, aged 85."

There is a faint, recorded recollection of Mr Wigglesworth (Robinson & Robinson) as a Wash guide, with his horse and long staff. And he was presumably buried at Long Sutton because Sutton Bridge church was not built until 1841/42. But why should a coalman have been a guide? Perhaps the link, once again, was the estuary. He had horses, his coal would have arrived by sailing vessels, and living on the west bank of the estuary he would have had an intimate knowledge of the tides.

Interestingly, Charles Wigglesworth evidently lived long enough to have seen the landscape swarming with navvies as the new channel for the river Nene was dug. He would have seen the causeway built and the opening of the first bridge at Sutton Bridge. In consequence, he must also have witnessed the knell of Wash guiding. Indeed, his death broke just about the last link between Long Sutton and the sea.

Memories of the Wellstream estuary (though some writers relate the name solely to the watercourse south of Wisbech) and its dangers go back much further than this, however. There is a record (Norman Wills. Fenland Churches & People. Wills, 1988) of an Elizabethan document of about 1600 which speaks of "sertaine guides who . . . conduct passengers." As for Shakespeare, he had King John (Act V, scene 6) lament:

> " . . . half my power this night
> Passing these flats, are taken by the tide,
> These Lincoln Washes, have devoured them,
> Myself, well-mounted, hardly have escap'd."

Also deeply ingrained in local lore were stories of hunters lured by the thought of lost jewels. Again, my father recounted some of the yarns. According to him there was the group in the 1930s which undertook a lengthy field-walking programme, ostensibly to find the jewels, and who - so the stories said - were nothing more than foreign spies mapping the area to plot paratroop dropping zones. And there was the local coroner who, in expectation of holding a famous inquest with the world and his dog watching, boned up on the law relating to Treasure Trove and asked the Home Office for advice on how to cope with the noisy demands of newspapermen and wireless and cine news crews.

It is possible to put a little flesh on one or two of these bones. John Seymour (East Anglia. Collins, revised 1988) pointed out that "some years ago" a Nottingham University team made a series of test borings near Walpole St Andrew and brought up metal scrapings. The matter is not at all clear, and the two projects may not be connected, but in 1988 (EDP, February 20) newspapers reported that Professor James Holt of Cambridge University had begun to study fragments of gold and silver brought up in the 1950s or 60s from a 30ft bore hole somewhere "south of Sutton Bridge."

Alan Bloom was less vague. He wrote that in 1906 the Daily Express reported that an "ancient loving cup" had been found at Gedney Drove End by a Wisbech publican digging for clams. The man sold it for a shilling and the new owner cleaned it, reckoned it silver, and found the date 1162 engraved on the bottom. Some of the treasure at last? Alas, no. Expert examination showed it to be the lacquered pewter bottom of an oil lamp, complete with its design number.

Bloom also recorded that in 1936 an American, said to be a millionaire (what else!), declared his determination to find King John's lost treasure and return it to the Crown. He formed a company and purchased Dovecote farm, opposite the church at Walpole St Peter, as a base. Drilling gear and detection equipment was brought in and offices, a photographic studio and a wireless communications room installed. Nearby farmers were paid for their trouble (2s 6d for every acre searched, I believe), and shafts sunk to 30ft in an attempt to locate the ancient causeway.

However, Bloom said the electrical detection equipment was incapable of handling the job, the team found only silt, and the project fizzled out. Another source recorded later that the only "find" was a changed strata of soil under a field of gooseberries.

In the 13th century the landscape between King's Lynn and Wisbech was a patchwork of fields, drove roads, greens, marshes, water courses, sea banks and long, muddy tracks. Many of the drove roads led to common pastures, shared by groups of villages, while the edges of the commons and greens were being increasingly settled. It was also a relatively rich region of Norfolk, though in truth life must always have been a struggle on both banks of an estuary which even today divides the sing-song dialects of Norfolk from the harsher tones of the inhabitants of South Lincolnshire.

Before drainage it must have been an even more bleak and forbidding place. On the west bank a ridge of higher land (Holland means "high land") supported scattered communities such as Tydd, Sutton, Lutton, Gedney, Fleet and Holbeach, and provided a line of communication from Boston, Swineshead and Spalding to the mouth of the estuary. On the opposite bank salt-producing communities such as Terrington, clinging to a lip of the estuary which jutted dangerously into the Wash, were notoriously vulnerable to flooding - and remained so for centuries - and they were still separated from Lynn by the old course of the Ouse. Lynn folk travelling to Wisbech, on the other hand, had to skirt the edges of The Lenn, the pool or lake from which Lynn got its name (the Welsh word llyn meaning pool or lake), and cross the Nar near Wiggenhall St Germans.

As for the rest it was birds and osiers, reed and sedge, fish and eels, marsh grazing in summer and wintering on the higher grasslands, fevers and the ague, mists, fogs and swamp gasses. It must have been an unremittingly grim existence.

Later writers added a little detail. Some fenmen were said to have used, first, stilts and later on vaulting poles to find their way across the creeks and watercourses. This is not quite as far-fetched as it sounds. In the late 1960s Percy Long, of Sutton St Edmund, revealed (Lincolnshire Free Press, cutting, undated, but possibly 1967-71) that some 40 years earlier he had found in the roof of his Broadgate Road home an old vaulting pole still inscribed with the initials of its previous owner, who is thought to have died in the 1860s. The pole, still in Percy's possession, was 15ft long and had a square block of wood at one end to prevent it sinking into the mud. It was evidently used to cross dikes, and Percy said he could remember men using poles when he was young.

To relieve the debilitating pains of the ague fen men traditionally used a number of remedies based on opium, or tea made from infusions of poppy seeds. Indeed, H J Mason (An Introduction to the Black Fens. Mason, 1973) recorded an old saying:

"Poppy tea and opium pill
Are the fen cure for many an ill."

These tough, rough, independent inhabitants - among whom, almost certainly, was a criminal element which had fled into the fens to escape justice - also came to be known as yellow-bellies (a watery existence, like frogs, perhaps, though I believe the opium habit does also induce a somewhat sallow complexion), slodgers (splashing through mud and water) or tigers (the ferocity with which they resisted early attempts at drainage). The names linger. Yellow-belly, I think, has come to mean anyone from South Lincolnshire, and the yellow and black-clad Holbeach United football team are known as the Tigers.

About AD1100 the available land surface became too small to support the growing communities, and they began to invest heavily in reclamation and the building of sea banks. The labour went on in stages until the protective and so-called "Roman" bank was finished, complete (or so aerial photography suggests, in at least one place) with breakwaters, and until many of the droves were created along with new parishes, hamlets and monastic granges. These constructions represented decades of astonishing and laborious effort by work gangs, presumably in conditions not too far removed from serfdom, and a heavy investment in terms of money, time and labour. Place-names like Walton, Walpole and Walsoken testify to years of labouring on the sea walls, and may even, in one dark interpretation, echo the use of slave labour. The Anglo Saxon word wahl, according to Bond, Penn and Rogerson (Norfolk Origins 4: The North Folk. Poppyland Publishing, 1990) meant foreigner or slave, and can be applied to these communities. Wahl may also have given us Walcott and Walsham.

One source says that between 1150 and 1300 the people of the villages around the Wash, and such "inland" communities as Wiggenhall, wrested some 16 square miles from the marshes and 90 square miles from the fens by building miles of banks and ditches. Parker & Pye (The Fenland. David & Charles, 1976) calculated that fen reclamations brought the new parishes to the very boundaries of Crowland which, incidentally, sparked a lawsuit to determine common rights on the marsh. The judgement ultimately went against the men of Holland, which some writers have interpreted as one of a number of local nails in King John's coffin.

At the time of John, however, Lynn, a small port squashed between the rivers Gay and Nar and divided by several smaller streams and fleets, was a dominant force in the locality. Corn, cloth and wool went out (to Newcastle, London, Gascony, France, Norway and the Baltic) while coal, fish, timber, furs and wine came in. As an example of local levels of trade, in 1203/4 Norwich collected nearly £7 customs dues and Yarmouth over £54, while the Lynn total was £651 11s 11d. In fact, in John's time only London and Southampton paid more duty than the Wash ports of Lynn and Boston.

The precise condition and boundaries of The Lenn at this time are not known, but David Higgins (Commons in Norfolk. Norfolk Research Committee, 1988) thinks that by 1086 it may have been an area of mud flats subject to occasional flooding. In earlier times The Lenn is thought to have stretched from the southern edge of present-day West Lynn as far as Wiggenhall St Germans, and from the

A peaceful modern scene at Foul Anchor.

outskirts of Tilney to the edge of West Winch. However, by early in the 13th century reclamation and defensive embankment work was already under way.

Any consideration of the events involving John's baggage train must inevitably take account of the question of crossing places over the main estuary, for crossing places there certainly were. There is the evidence of the Wigglesworth tombstone, already mentioned. And I have a copy of a letter written by the Rev H F Rushmer, of Foulden (EDP, undated cutting) in which he recounted a story told by a certain John Bailey, a native of Walpole St Peter, who died in 1921, that his step-sister was drowned crossing the Wash one evening in a storm. "It appears a man kept two horses to do the journey, one for himself and the other for his passenger, and regularly escorted people back and forth," he wrote.

This story is puzzling because the causeway, which provided a safe crossing place, opened in 1831. Mr Rushmer also recounted another tale by a Titchwell man, then deceased, who had told him that according to time and tide it was once possible to ride out (into the Wash, presumably) nine miles on horseback "without the water coming above the horse's barrel."

It has long been assumed there was a crossing place near Walsoken, where the estuary was at its narrowest, or at least, where the road to Wisbech allowed safe passage. Faden's map of 1797 also marks a ford between West Walton and Newton just south of Ferry House. Even when this map was drawn, there was no bridge across the estuary until Wisbech was reached. There is also a school of thought which believes in a causeway in the vicinity of Walpole St Peter, with west bank landfall in the vicinity of Tydd Gote and Foul Anchor.

By far the most important in recent history, however, was the route beginning on the east bank at Cross Keys, site of a subsidiary community belonging to Walpole St Andrew which grew up on the old main road and the sea bank. Faden marked this route "Wash Way fordable at Low Water" and showed it leading to Cross Keys House (formerly Wash House, now the Bridge Hotel at Sutton Bridge) and indeed, called the estuary Cross Keys Wash. White's Norfolk Directory of 1845 (David & Charles, 1969) also called it Cross Keys Wash, recalling that "the only passage between the two counties was by a precarious road or track, two miles in length, across the sands which were left nearly dry at low water."

It also recalled how in 1825 an Act was passed to build a bridge - called Sutton's Bridge - over the new Nene channel and a "high embanked road" across the broad Wash. It went on to add that the scheme recovered 15,000 acres of land from the estuary. The bank alone took 900 men over three years to build.

It is interesting to note (Stafford Linsley, article. Norfolk Archaeology, vol XL11, pt 1. Norfolk & Norwich Archaeological Society, 1994) that in 1780 Joseph Oxley, a bottle salesman from Hartley, Northumberland, travelling on horseback, arrived on the banks of the estuary from Spalding, on his way to Lynn Regis, in late December. He reached Lynn on New Year's Day, 1781, having made the long detour to Wisbech. It might have been a business opportunity that took him into Cambridgeshire, of course. On the other hand he may simply have taken fright at the idea of a winter crossing of the dangerous estuary.

A further hint of the historical importance of the site of Cross Keys as one end of a crossing route is the possibility of a Roman road extending from the old shore of the estuary all the way to West Lynn and Lynn, and even on into central Norfolk. In Terrington St Clement Through the Ages (H Ward, 1974) the author commented that early on the only metalled road, "probably of Roman origin," was that which ran through the village to Lynn and east to the shore. It is a much debated highway. East Anglian Archaeology (No 5, 1977) described it as a continuation of the Roman road from Billingford and Gayton which led out of Lynn along Ferry Lane and thence to Wash Lane, Clenchwarton, and Terrington. Six years later Robinson & Rose (Roads and Tracks. Poppyland, 1983), merely described it as a "possible" Roman road running from Brisley to Lynn, adding: "It has been suggested it may have continued as far as Cowbit, near Spalding."

The Clenchwarton field survey, 1988, on the other hand, reported there was "no evidence" of Roman activity in the area and that the identification of a Roman road through the village "carries little conviction." Then again, An Historical Atlas of Norfolk (Norfolk Museums Service, 1993) showed the road on its Roman map and listed it as "probable."

Whatever the origins of this particular road, the importance of Cross Keys as a terminus is not in dispute. Even so, the natural conclusion that a 13th century crossing route must perforce have made landfall on the opposite bank at the present site of Sutton Bridge - as the route does today - is open to challenge. Sutton Bridge as a community of substance did not exist then, for the area it now covers was, at the time of John, part of the estuary tidal plains. Only in the late 1700s did the village began to take shape. In addition Long Sutton, which was once lapped by the waters of the Wash, is probably not on its original site. Indeed, it may have developed from an earlier community sited further to the south.

Long Sutton church steeple glimpsed from Sutton Crosses.

There are two possible clues to this. One is the suggestion (Robinson & Robinson) that an early community called Dolproun, which may have preceded the development of Long Sutton, once existed in the Peterspoint area. Presumably no more than a collection of huts (W H Wheeler. History of the Fens of South Lincolnshire. Newcomb, 1894), it was said to have been washed away in 1236.

This is difficult to understand. Dolproun could have been pre-Roman conquest, of course, when sea levels were different, but by the 13th century Petherspoint was covered by the tides. Perhaps it was a group of fishermen's huts; on the other hand the name might refer not to a community but to a bank which was breached and flooded, forcing folk to move marginally north on to higher ground.

The second clue (Robinson & Robinson) is that in circa AD1120 Robert de Haia gave land for the purpose of erecting a church at Sutton. This was built of wood, thatched, and as far as is known lasted about 50 years. When the foundations of the "new" stone church were laid - on a higher and more northerly site - in about 1180, instructions were given that the "old" church was to be pulled down and the bodies buried there transferred to the new cemetery. In this new position, high tide meant the sea was only half a mile or so away.

For reasons which are not entirely relevant to this story, my father (Robinson & Robinson) was convinced the wooden church, probably the focal point of the original Sutton community, was sited near the junction of Station Road and Oldgate, formerly known as Sutton Two Crosses or Sutton Cross End, and now as Sutton Crosses. This meant that Seagate road, which is very old, would have led from the village to the estuary.

It adds weight to the idea that the Cross Keys route originally made landfall on the west bank near Sutton Crosses, which is slightly to the south of the present route to Sutton Bridge. At Sutton Crosses, the Manor House, possibly near Seagate, would undoubtedly have been a prominent landmark. And at such an important crossing place, one can only speculate that there might also have been a rest house and stables in the vicinity.

King John may have known this area reasonably well. One report suggested he was among a list of subscribers who supported the building of Sutton's "new" church. In 1202 it is possible he was in the area as he granted the village a market charter, thus initiating the development of the new site (as opposed to Sutton Crosses) as the more important community. At some point he also granted Lordship of the Manor of Sutton Holland to Gerard Camville, and enjoyed the influence of the de Haia family. Again, on October 8, 1205, he is said to have signed a Long Sutton document and a Lynn document on the very same day. He presumably crossed the estuary in the process.

Clearly, he was among friends amid the merchants and ship owners at Lynn. It was John's charter which had made this port a "free burgh," with powers to control its own waterborne goods, a move which not only enabled it to expand but also laid the foundation of the town's Royalist leanings.

Incidentally, this suggestion of constant travelling should come as no surprise. In John's time there was no fixed place of parliament, no permanent royal residence. Government was where the king happened to be. Therefore, the king's travelling household was a sort of national capital constantly on the move, for as he travelled he signed decrees, made laws, decided policy and doled out justice. John, for example, is thought to have shifted his residence on average a dozen times a month, rarely staying anywhere for more than two or three days at a time. And it was certainly not unusual for the king and his party to separate from the baggage train. Indeed, and with a royal party on faster horses and unencumbered by wagons and loads, one can almost believe that for most of the time the baggage train scarcely knew where the king was.

The details of John's turbulent early life - he has been described as short and stout, possessing a volatile temper and a sardonic sense of humour, a snappy dresser, gourmet and a womaniser - are scarcely relevant here, but it is worth recalling that in 1214 the barons, by this time thoroughly disenchanted with him, decided to call a meeting to discuss what to do. With an element of secretiveness they chose Bury St Edmunds, for its remoteness and for its famous shrine, using a St Edmunds' Day pilgrimage as cover for the journey and the gathering. At the meeting the Archbishop of Canterbury, Stephen Langton, treading the delicate line of a peace-maker, placed before the barons a Charter of Liberties which, after the events at Runnymede in 1215, was to become known as Magna Carta.

That same year, 1215, John was to issue writs to monastic and other houses to gather up his possessions "such as vessels, jewels, gold and silver and others." The price of his ambition, and the cost of mercenary troops, was beginning to catch up with the exchequer.

By 1216 the country was torn by civil war and John, faced by problems of great complexity, went on the offensive perhaps in the belief that, as Winston Churchill put it (A History of the English Speaking Peoples, vol 1. Cassell, 1956), "there seemed to be every chance (that he) would still defeat the baronial opposition and wipe out the humiliation of Runnymede." Until Louis of France landed, that is. Then John, angry and desperate and backed by a hired army of foreign mercenaries, "burst like a whirlwind on the east, ravaging the shires." In the west a number of barons remained loyal, and a number of key castles including Windsor and Dover also stood for the crown. Nichola de la Haia also remained loyal at Lincoln, and Lynn was a staunch ally, too.

In September, John marched to Crowland where he is said to have attempted to fire the abbey church and where he did manage to destroy the harvest fields. Then he went to Grimsby, possibly to arrange for the receipt of stores and equipment to be shipped later from Lynn, and on to Lincoln, where he is thought to have stayed until about October 2. After that it was south again, through Boston (October 5) and Spalding (October 7 and 8), burning as he went. Then on Sunday, October 9, 1216, he and his mercenaries and baggage train, sumpter horses, wagons and carts, reached Lynn, which means he could have crossed the estuary again (the journey via Wisbech would have added 20 miles) and could even have taken advantage of the de la Haia connection and stayed overnight in Sutton prior to the crossing in order to catch low tide.

His reasons for wanting to be in Lynn may have been two-fold. Lauded and welcomed by the commercial classes he would have been among supporters. And it is presumed there was an urgent need for him to arrange for the shipment of supplies to strongholds further north. In the event the citizens of Lynn feasted him well. Too well, perhaps, for John evidently over-indulged. Finally, exhausted by stress and many days of hard riding, he became seriously ill with dysentery.

From this point on there is a sharp rise in the level of conjecture, but the salient facts seem to be these: John was at Lynn on Tuesday, October 11; Wisbech and Swineshead on October 12; Sleaford on October 14 and 15; and lying ill at Newark on October 16 and 17. He died next day.

It is also worth looking at some of the historical accounts of the disaster. The extraordinary Matthew Paris (writer, artist, monk, historian and precious metal worker, who died in 1259) recorded: "Leaving the town of Lynn . . . he (John) attempted to force a passage over the water which is called the Welle stream, and there suddenly and irrecoverably lost all his wagons, treasures, costly goods and regalia. A whirlpool in the middle of the water absorbed all into its depths, with men and horses, so that hardly one escaped to announce the misfortune to the King." He added that the baggage train had attempted to cross without a guide. At one time the Ouse and the Nene joined forces inland of Wisbech, being called the Wellstream, but the party is unlikely to have crossed here, so far off its known route. The implication is that the name Welle, in general use, meant the estuary as a whole.

Ralph, abbot of Coggeshall, said the incident occurred at the Wellstream "because they had set out incautiously and hastily before the tide had receded." This latter comment may be important because it implies a morning crossing. As for Roger of Wendover, he described it as an "unexpected accident" with the King "barely escaping with his army" and spending "the following night" at Swineshead.

Interpretations of these records, seen against the background of John's known movements, have been many and varied over the years. In 1906 W St John Hope (Archaeologia) suggested that John and his army went to Swineshead via Wisbech while the baggage train, in attempting to shorten the journey by using the Cross Keys route, started late and was caught in quicksands. Four decades later this was challenged by Gordon Fowler (Proceedings of the Cambridge Antiquarian Society, 1953) who could find no evidence of quicksand and who was convinced that in the early 13th century the estuary was not passable at all north of Wisbech. He argued that the entire party was obliged to pass through or near to Wisbech and that the loss came when they forded the Wellstream between Walsoken and Wisbech, where the estuary was only a quarter of a mile wide. The accident, he thought, was probably caused by a sudden tidal surge.

Eight years later Prof J C Holt (Nottingham Medieval Studies, 1961) did record some evidence of quicksand in medieval levels near the natural causeway. He himself believed that the party had attempted to cross between Walpole and what is now Tydd Gote, close to Foul Anchor, a name doubtless significant in terms of treacherous waters. Rodney Tibbs also argued in favour of a crossing site somewhere between Wisbech and Walsoken, adding that this is where the treasure, "if it exists," would lie. R G Walpole (The Walpole Villages and Other People. Regency Press, 1979), on the other hand, made no bones about where he would concentrate his search - "it would be to the east of Walpole Bank, now signposted East Bank, where the land is still very soggy today at a wet time."

My father (Robinson & Robinson) believed the baggage train left Lynn on October 11 in order to leave Cross Keys at low water the following day and that John, meanwhile, rode to Wisbech to complete his business - one school of thought has it that the group of Lynn ship owners handling John's supplies happened to be in Wisbech at the time, or had gone there purposely to avoid him - and then, perhaps pausing at Sutton on the way to Swineshead, was either told of the disaster or watched the drama from the safety of the west bank as it unfolded in mid-estuary.

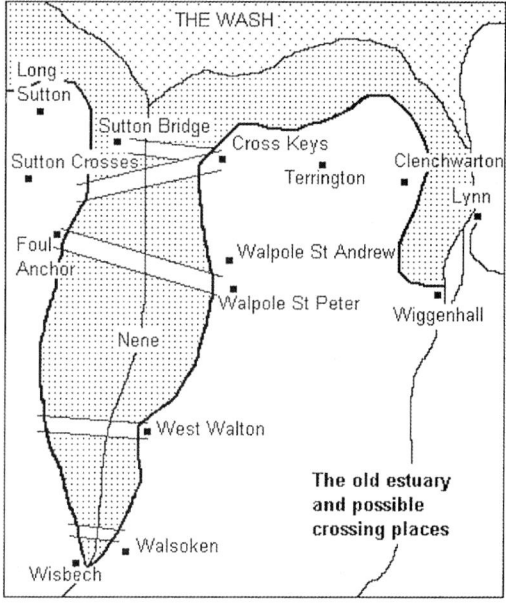

He also introduced the interesting idea that John's ardent supporter, Nichola de la Haia, heroine of the siege of Lincoln, might possibly have been in Sutton at the time. There is no evidence to support the suggestion, but he pointed out that South Holland's courts baron main meeting was invariably held shortly after the Feast of St Michael. In South Lincolnshire in more recent times, for civil purposes, Michaelmas was treated as the old quarter day, October 11.

Perhaps we now have the framework of what happened during those two dramatic days. John was desperate to conclude his business with the Lynn ship owners and to hurry north again, but he may have found that (W L Warren), whether through ill luck, shrewd foresight or commercial misjudgement, the very men he wanted to see (said to have been Ralph FitzWalter, Godfrey le Pohier, Osbert Fitzwalter, Benedict de Beautre, Thomas de Beautre, William the German, Reginald But and John FitzAlan) were indeed away on business in Wisbech. But John, thoroughly out of sorts and quite ill and yet aware of how urgently supplies were needed in the north, was anxious to tie up loose ends and get on the road.

My construction of events would be that early on Tuesday, October 11 (sunrise about 6.25am, low water about noon, it is thought) the baggage train, with at least some of the foot soldiers acting as "shotgun," left Lynn bound for Cross Keys. The plan was either that John and his officials and bodyguard, able to move much faster than the wagons, would ride to Wisbech, complete the business, and meet the baggage train on the other side of the estuary; or that both groups would rest overnight, John in Wisbech and the baggage train on the bank at Cross Keys, and meet up the following morning.

In view of John's fatigue and his debilitating illness, the latter seems more logical while the former, even if the baggage train could have reached Sutton Crosses before the turn of the day's tide, would have left John with his negotiations with the boat owners on top of something like 20 miles of hard riding, in winter, on muddy tracks. It is questionable, in his condition, if he could have completed all this and reached Sutton Crosses in time to meet the convoy.

Another factor sometimes overlooked, which also seems to support the overnight theory, is the length of time the baggage train might have needed to travel from Lynn to Cross Keys. It may have used the old Roman road through Clenchwarton, if Roman road it was, but there was still the initial problem of crossing the channel to West Lynn. Estimates of the size of John's party vary, but it is thought to have included something like 2500 to 3000 knights, crossbow men and mercenaries, and a baggage train of horses, oxen, springless wagons and carts.

Charles Kightly (see below) has described some of the baggage trains of medieval kings, and the chaos and pandemonium which must have surrounded them like a cloud. At any given time such a column might have included members of the household and travelling civil servants, the chief minister (chancellor), steward (who supervised kitchen and larder), butler (who kept everyone supplied with wine), chamberlain (responsible for the king's travelling bed chamber), treasurer (who kept the accounts), staff (including washerwomen, a tailor and a bathman), constables and marshals (who maintained law and order in a travelling household), and sumptermen, responsible for packing and transportation.

Everything, including the tents, had to be folded into saddlebags or stowed in a sumpter, a chest for carriage on a packhorse or wagon. Valuable and fragile items, which might have included the king's wardrobe and possessions, may have warranted a four-wheeled wagon. Ladies were sometimes carried on swaying litters slung between two horses, rode in elaborate carriages, or on their own horse. Not surprisingly, most members of the court preferred to ride, perhaps on a palfrey (a quiet, well-bred horse) or a rouncy, which was stronger. Some of the ladies rode astride on a small jennet, while richer clerks had a good mule and lesser folk a hackney, or a spare packhorse.

The train, a hubbub of carts and wagons, packhorses and pack-saddles, panniers and falcons, dogs and crowds of people, must have been an impressive sight on the move, but a column could have travelled only at little more than walking pace, say 3-4mph. In the best of conditions John's train would surely have taken nearly three hours to move from West Lynn to Cross Keys. But this was in October, when travelling conditions were likely to be bad, and it had to get to West Lynn first.

How long did this crossing take? Was there a ford, or were they ferried? With low water not due until about noon, either the column was ferried across (a long and frustrating business, no doubt, particularly with animals and carts) or it waited until midday (assuming the tide predictions are correct). Either way, a same day crossing to Sutton Crosses looks less and less likely.

King John may have seen something of this and then hurried off to Wisbech, his temper scarcely salved, leaving orders that he would meet the column at Sutton Crosses on the morrow. Presumably accompanied by an armed escort and by assorted clerks to do the legal work, he may have ridden through West Winch and Setch and then west to Wiggenhall St Germans. From here, he could have gone by way of Lordsbridge to Tilney St Lawrence and thence on the higher ground to Walsoken along The Highway. Once at Wisbech, perhaps at a later hour than he planned, John turned in for the night. The baggage train, meanwhile, reached Cross Keys, also later than expected, and settled down.

Early next morning, increasingly ill and fatigued, John completed his business with the Lynn ship owners and then rode from Wisbech to Sutton Crosses to await the baggage train.

If guides were in attendance on the baggage train they would surely have counselled against a crossing of the Wellstream - at either Cross Keys or somewhere in the vicinity of Walpole (for it it always possible the baggage train declined the West Lynn crossing, and forded the river at Wiggenhall instead) - before the tide had fully turned. Perhaps October mists and fogs wrapped the estuary in silence and obscured the dangers posed by a partially retreated tide. Or was there even a hint of local sabotage here? Either way, the thought of an angry John waiting on the far bank seems to have spurred the baggage masters into beginning the crossing before the waters had fully receded.

The rest is history. Most accounts seem to agree that the wagons and horses and some of the men got into trouble amid the creeks and streams and the sucking sand and mud. It must have been an appalling scene, but it is possible some escaped and perhaps struggled across to the Lincolnshire side or back to the Norfolk bank. In view of comments that John himself "barely escaped," it may be that he attempted to organise some sort of rescue which had to be abandoned as the tide turned again. The timing element is against this. He still faced a ride of something like 25 miles to Swineshead, which he apparently reached on time. But he may at least have witnessed the disaster.

What, precisely, was lost? Nothing is known of the loss of life involved. There has been rather more speculation about the jewels. Warren says that between May, 1215, and March, 1216, John gathered in great quantities of his jewels, plate and regalia from monastic houses, presumably to pay his troops. Thus much of his original hoard may have been pawned or sold prior to the disaster. The regalia of the Empress Matilda was never heard of again after 1216, and was perhaps lost, though there is another story it was stolen at Newark while John was on his death bed.

Ravensdale & Muir commented that the "quicksand consumed waggons and escort, and Plantagenet regalia, scores of drinking vessels of gold and silver, and the king's personal collection of gemstones." Somewhat more soberly, Coggeshall recorded that John lost "his chapel with his relics and some packhorses with divers household effects." In other words, he downgraded the event. Some of the effects may, in any event, have been surreptitiously recovered by canny fen men making use of local knowledge and the next low tide.

King John, no doubt anguished by the loss of the column, struggled on to Swineshead where, that evening, he dined with the abbot. One account says he enjoyed peaches and new cider. On October 14 and 15, increasingly sick and by now carried by litter, he rested at Sleaford before finally struggling on to the Bishop of Lincoln's castle at Newark. He could go no further. The Abbot of Croxton, who had a reputation for medical skills, was summoned, but on October 18, his strength ebbing but his mind evidently as clear as a bell, John dictated his will and declared his son Henry as his heir. The abbot heard his confession and performed last rites. King John died later that night, when a gale is said to have rattled the rooftops of the town.

There are a number of stories related to his death, but the most widely accepted is that he died of dysentery aggravated by fatigue and too much food and drink. One version adds that the dysentery was brought on by a feast of lampreys at Lynn. There are also at least three poisoning theories. One story relates this dark act to Swineshead, where John may not have been a particularly welcome guest. The monks of Swineshead were Cistercians and John, over the years, had "hurtfully molested" the brother abbeys of Peterborough and Crowland.

Yet another version pins local resentment firmly on the reclaimed commons boundaries lawsuit at Crowland. Parker & Pye (The Fenland. David & Charles, 1976) commented that "the decision, which went against the men of Holland, did not endear King John to them, and the true cause of his death after spending a night at Swineshead abbey in 1216 remains uncertain to this day."

Essentially, the versions of the poisoning theory are these: 1, the abbot had a good-looking sister and became upset at her being subjected to the king's insensitive amusement; 2, John, in a thoroughly bad temper because of illness and the events of the day, swore he would cause the price of bread to rise; and 3, that a monk named Simon prepared a poisoned drink and gave it to the king. The king insisted that Simon drink first, which he did. Simon then retired to his cell and died. The king, though ill, managed to reach Newark before dying. "For years afterwards it was said masses were offered for the soul of Brother Simon," one account says.

But these are side issues. The more interesting mystery, it seems to me, is the one surrounding the events of October 11 and 12, 1216. The Sutton Wellstream, now relegated to the size of a pond, has so far kept its secrets. Even the estuary has been obliterated, and the fen fogs that still sometimes blanket the land continue to obscure the reality of the events of 780 years ago.

As a postscript, not until 1829 did work start on digging the present Nene outfall, at a cost of many lives and waves of cholera and smallpox in the locality. On May 5, 1831, the new river banks were completed and at noon the Wash tide ceased to flow over Sutton Wash and up the Wellstream estuary.

In July of that same year the Union coach from Norwich to Newark, watched by hundreds of excited spectators, made the first passage by wheeled transport over the new causeway from Cross Keys to Sutton Bridge. The causeway, still with its road on top, is now an abandoned relic having been superseded by a newer, lower A17. In its time, however, it shortened the journey from Norfolk into Lincolnshire and the Midlands by many miles and hours.

SELECTED REFERENCES AND READING

Astbury, A K. The Black Fens. EP Publishing, 1958.
Bloom, Alan. The Fens. Hale, 1953.
Faden's Map of Norfolk, 1797. Larks Press edition, 1989.
Hallam, H E. Rural England, 1066-1348. Fontana, 1981.
Kightly and Cyprien. A Travellers' Guide to Royal Roads. Historical Times Inc and RKP, 1985.
Margeson, Seillier and Rogerson. The Normans in Norfolk. Norfolk Museums Service, 1994.
Ordnance Survey. Landranger map 131, Boston & Spalding area. OS, 1992.
Ravensdale and Muir. East Anglian Landscapes. Joseph, 1984.
Richards, Paul. King's Lynn. Phillimore, 1990.
Robinson, F W and B A. History of Long Sutton & District. Long Sutton Civic Trust, 1981 (reprinted 1995).
The Fenland Project, No 3, Norfolk Survey, Marshland and Nar Valley. East Anglian Archaeology, 1988.
Tibbs, Rodney. Fenland River. Terence Dalton, 1969.
Warren, W L. King John. Peregrin Books, 1966.

PLACES TO VISIT

King's Lynn (the museum in Market Street, Town House Museum in Queen Street) and Wisbech offer glimpses of fen and marshland life in times past; while many of the fine churches (Terrington St Clement, Walpole St Peter and St Andrew, Walsoken, Long Sutton, etc) have a bold style and flavour of their own. It is worth getting an OS map and exploring these places by car, seeking out the old sea banks and the flat, windswept country on both sides of the former estuary - the Walpoles, West Walton, Foul Anchor, Tydd St Mary, Peterspoint, Sutton Crosses and Long Sutton.

> *Sometime during the night of August 26/27, 1549, the thousands of rebels camped on Mousehold Heath overlooking the city of Norwich set fire to their shelters and marched off into the darkness. They were leaving behind them a virtually impregnable position, choosing to face a smaller, disciplined army of professional fighters out in the open, on the rolling slopes of the heath. Clearly, it was meant to be the final, decisive confrontation. But why did Robert Kett choose to bring matters to a head, to provoke a battle he must have suspected he might lose? Was it bravado, or had he simply run out of options?*

5: *The* Great Commotion

One of the enduring aspects of the ultimately grisly Kett Rebellion of 1549 is its accessibility. After nearly 450 years you can still touch it. It is still possible to stroll around Wymondham, where it began; stand beside Kett's Oak near Hethersett, where the rebels gathered; tramp the slopes of the heath near Gas Hill, Norwich, and the place where Kett had his great camp; visit Bishopgate Bridge and Holmstrete, now Bishopgate, attacked and fired by the rebels on a number of occasions; and gaze at Norwich castle ramparts, where it all ended with such predictable civic brutality.

Another charm, I think, is the slow metamorphosis of the leading player, in the public mind, from enemy of the state to local hero. It has not been easy and it has taken a long time, but Robert Kett, landowner, encloser, man of property, somehow managed to straddle the camps of the popular and the propertied and has emerged if not the hero of both then at least as a man who tried to right a number of wrongs but who paid the inevitable penalty for his presumption.

It would be a grave mistake, however, to see him as a latter day Robin Hood. Both came to be seen as symbols of hope during miserable times, but most of the similarities end there. Hood was and still is a hazy figure of lore and myth, perhaps even an amalgam of a number of stories. Kett was no ghost. He was flesh and blood, a perceivable man of substance. So when did the change come? When did his persona undergo radical transformation and a largely hostile Establishment give his memory the gloss of heroism? It is hard to say, but it might have been during the 19th century, at the time of Empire, when, by coincidence, Boudica was also taken off the shelf, dusted down, and seen in a bright, new patriotic light. Consider these comments:

"The said Erl (Warwick), upon Musholde Hethe, vanquyshed Robert Kette and his hool number of adherents, of their most wicked rebellion, and did suppresse them and delivered this Cittie from the great daunger, trouble and peril it was in . . . " (The Norwich City Book, 1549).

". . . the said Kett wolde by his sinister will with his adherents command eny unlawfull thing to bee done in the contry . . . Then the seid wretched Kett by force made the seid Thomas Codd, Mayour, and Thomas Aldrich aforesayd & Robert Watson to bee apprehendid in the Cyttie. . . Whylst theis things were a doing in the Cyttie, Kett did sent abroade by his Embassators to rayse the whole Country, by which means resortid to him a greate numbre . . ." (Nicholas Sotherton, circa 1559).

" . . . vile Rabble, the Scum and Dregs of Norfolk and Suffolk." (Alexander Neville. The Norfolk Furies. 1575).

"Thus perished, with its authors, this desperate rebellion, which threatened the subversion of all lawful authority, and the consequent introduction of anarchy and confusion." (White's 1845 Norfolk).

"The rebels . . . tell us, what indeed we may learn from a thousand other instances, that the end does not justify the means; that a cause, however just in itself, can never prosper if it be not lawfully and quietly won . . . " (Rev Henry Nevill, lecture, 1857).

"We cherish the memory of men who have died for less than this (Kett's list of grievances) and call them martyrs!" (W A Dutt. Highways & Byways in East Anglia. Macmillan, 1932 edition, first edition 1901).

"In reparation and honour to a noble and courageous leader in the struggles of the common people of England to escape from a servile life to the freedom of present conditions." (Plaque on Norwich Castle wall, erected 1949).

Of course, the above extracts are hardly comprehensive and prove little, but they do help to illustrate the reappraisal and huge shift in opinion which has taken place. For example, it is a fair bet the 1949 plaque unveiling ceremony was attended by representatives of the City Council, essentially the same body which, 400 years before, had bought barrels of beer and rolled them out in the market place for the pleasure of victorious troops returning from the slaughter at Dussindale.

But it can also be argued that we are still no nearer a real understanding of the events of that summer, or of the man whose name local history has now stamped indelibly on the year 1549.

At the heart of the story the central enigma remains. Why did a man who built fences decide to help the mob pull them down? What were the factors which caused a successful and respected Wymondham businessman to change almost overnight, or so it would seem, into the leader of an angry band of peasants heading for Norwich and an inevitable collision with the law?

The complexity of Kett the man is mirrored by the complexity of his times. Henry V111 had left his throne to a child of nine, with all the political difficulties that implies, but the country had been in turmoil even before this. Henry's extravagances had already contributed to economic chaos. Coinage was debased, bad harvests had sent the price of food rocketing, inflation was rife. In the countryside, villages were failing, commons enclosures were bringing about evictions, and land speculation was creating large and less labour-intensive sheep farms, often on former monastic lands. It was a time of poverty, uncertainty and shifting fortunes.

There were other tangled threads in the story, too. Edward V1's Council appointed Hertford (later the Duke of Somerset) as Protector, turned out the leading Catholics and repealed an Act which allowed the King, on coming of age, to revoke statutes passed during the minority. Thus throughout 1548/49 ecclesiastical reformers were drawn to England, signalling the beginning of decades of conflict between Church and State. In essence, the "justified" church stressed pulpit and congregation rather than altar and priest.

In London (Keith Feiling. A History of England. Redwood Press, 1966), "congregations were taking down images, whitewashing walls, selling vestments to City tailors, while at Portsmouth others were breaking down altars . . . " Then early in 1549 Cranmer and others produced the first prayerbook from Catholic and Protestant sources. The first full English service was held in January, 1549.

Of course, it might be argued that religious turmoil was little more than one element in the background to the Kett Rebellion, and in a sense this seems to have been true. With one important exception, Wymondham Abbey, of which more later. Most commentators, however, seem to agree the real culprits were sheep.

In Norfolk, weaving was important and Norwich, with a population of about 10,000, had become the centre for an increasingly large population of gentry. Between 1525/69, for example, the number of freemen in distribution and clothing (grocers, the richest and most influential group; haberdashers, tailors, cordwainers) nearly quadrupled, while the number of those engaged in textiles remained largely static. At the same time, the export of worsted had declined, hitting craftsmen, builders and weavers. There were fortunes to be made and lost.

In the countryside there were also several layers of unease. The best profits (Land, see below) were going to those who farmed large enclosed tracts of land and who invested in large flocks raised with much reduced labour costs. In the eyes of labourers, some without homes or jobs, enclosure by wealthy landlords was despicable and the cause of much anger; but enclosure for the specific purpose of raising sheep was particularly resented. Not only were peasants losing use of the land being enclosed, but the system also rendered their labour cheap or redundant.

The level of bitterness seems to have increased in parallel with an increase in the size of the flocks. Land lists several local landowning examples. In 1521 the Fermors of East Barsham had some 17,000 sheep; and in 1551 Southwell of Wood Rising had 13,000. Between 1544 and 1548, Townshend of Raynham increased his sheep numbers from 3000 to 4200, while the wealth of the Heydons of Baconsthorpe and Saxlingham was largely based on the conversion of land to sheep.

So there was an extensive package of grievances, aside from the religious convulsions also gripping parts of the country. The money system was creaking, inflation was rife, leaseholders were being evicted and rights on commons nibbled away. Landlords were over-stocking with sheep as the price of wool rose, driving off the peasants' animals. Conversely, farm jobs were being cut and journeymen replaced by cheap apprentice labour. Inevitably, charity offerings fell and the plight of the landless poor increased. Despite Somerset's efforts, Parliament regularly voted down measures to improve the lot of the poverty-stricken and put a brake on evictions.

Inevitably, there was trouble. Locally, Land mentions a disturbance at Fakenham in 1520 relating to Sir Henry Germor's sheep walks, and a riot at Hingham in 1539 over Sir Henry Parker's enclosures. In 1540 there was an attempted rising against the gentry at Griston, and four years later riots at Great Dunham. Then about a year before the Kett rising, commoners gathered at Castle Rising and at Middleton, constituting a potential threat to King's Lynn.

These disputes all had common agricultural backgrounds. But in Devon and Cornwell there were riots against religious changes and the new English prayerbook. East Anglia, on the other hand, seems in general to have liked the "new" preachers and the English service, there being only a brief early flowering of sympathy for the Catholic cause.

Oddly, and according to Ravensdale & Muir, the first riots of the eastern rebellion occurred on June 20, 1549, at Wilby, only three miles from Kenninghall where Princess Mary, later Queen Mary, focus of hope for supporters of the Old Religion, happened to be residing. Most experts agree, however, that she was probably not involved in these particular troubles. On this occasion (Land) people from Attleborough, Eccles and Wilby attacked fences enclosing the common at Hargham and Attleborough, erected by John Green, lord of the manor of Wilby. But at Wymondham, and in addition to the problem of local enclosures and the rising cost of food, there was also the little difficulty of the Abbey church.

Wymondham's church had been shared by the monks and the parishioners for many years, and there had been numerous disputes, largely over matters of rights

Kett and his men on the Wymondham town sign beside Becket's chapel, now the library; with the Green Dragon pub on the left.

and upkeep. In 1534, however, the town's abbot and 10 monks submitted to the oath of supremacy, and the closure of their house was agreed in 1536. For 10 years the lands were held by the Crown; then four years before the Kett rising the site of the abbey and the manor of Wymondham were granted to Henry Howard, Earl of Surrey. The monastery was scheduled for demolition under the supervision of the local Crown Agent, John Flowerdew, who seems to have set about the task with particular zeal. It sparked much local resentment.

To begin with, many of the congregation feared that Flowerdew's enthusiasm for demolition might damage their part of the church, and they asked the King's permission to buy those portions of the monastery which were also structurally part of the church. The request was granted. Nevertheless, Flowerdew persisted.

There were also suspicions that Flowerdew, a rising and ambitious lawyer who owned land at Hethersett and who lived for a time at Stanfield Hall, three miles south of Hethersett, was turning the operation into a very profitable enterprise. Flowerdew's connection with Stanfield Hall, whose most famous resident was the luckless Amy Robsart, then aged 17 (Bartle Frere), was through family.

Flowerdew's brother had married one of Amy's half-sisters, which suggests that in the dispute over the demolition the Robsart family was probably on Flowerdew's side.

It was the aspect of profit, as several writers have pointed out, which may have been of particular annoyance to Kett, himself a man with an eye for business and one who might well have competed with Flowerdew for the job of demolition. Indeed, and according to A & A Hoare, Kett was one of the leading figures among a group of townsfolk who petitioned the King to save parts of the church for the town, including the steeple, bells, stone, lead, choir, vestry and Lady Chapel. Much was saved, including Becket's chapel, but Flowerdew seems to have pushed his enterprise to very limit.

Robert Kett was born in 1492, the fourth son of Tom and Margery Kett, whose family had been prominent in Wymondham for several generations. For some time the surname was various spelled as Kett, Ket, Cat, Chat and Knight. Kett seems to have been the most popular interpretation, and today's local telephone directories show a healthy modern survival of the name in the locality. However, Robert's great-grandfather, Richard, who held property in the Dykebeck and Chapelgate areas and was Alderman of the Guild of the Nativity of the Blessed Virgin, had evidently been born out of wedlock, so male descendants of the line often bore the name "Kett alias Knight."

Robert's father, Tom, farmed land at several places including Forncett, Tacolneston and Silfield, and leased other lands from the abbey. He was a butcher by trade and a member of the town Guild. Robert's brother, William, was a butcher and grazier with land at Forncett, and a mercer (a dealer in textiles) with shops in Chapelgate, near Becket's chapel, and two properties in Damgate. He was also an active churchman, having responsibility for some of the ornaments and candles in the Abbey church. It was William who purchased Westwode chapel in the manor of Choseley, where a cell of the Order of St Lazarus of Jerusalem had earlier been established, from the Earl of Warwick in 1545.

In 1519 Robert Kett, a leading member of the Guild of St Thomas the Martyr and an abbey server, married Alice Appleyard of Braconash. They had five sons, one of whom was given the name Loye, after Loye Ferrers, the last abbot of Wymondham who became vicar of Wymondham after the Dissolution. Kett is usually described as a tanner, though this may mean he held the manorial rights to tanning. Between 1530 and 1548 Robert is known to have been involved in a number of property transactions involving up to 90 acres of land and six properties. At various times (Hoare) he held land at Browick, near Stanfield, Suton, and near The Lizard. He also owned a three-acre meadow, and when the abbey was dissolved Robert was one of several local people who bought some of the land. In town, his properties seem to have been principally on the north side of Becket's chapel, Middleton, Cavick and Ton (Town) Green.

His house may have been on the south side of the Tiffey meadows near Becket's Well, though the Rev Nevill claimed Kett's house, though much altered and modernised, was still standing in 1857 and was known as Dykebeck.

At the inquest (Norwich Guildhall, January 13, 1550) following his execution, Kett's property was said to have consisted of the manor of Wymondham, some lands belonging to the Hospital of Burton Lazars, Leicestershire - both obtained, oddly as things turned out, from the Earl of Warwick - two tenements at Cakewyk Field near the marl pits, possibly close to Becket's Well, some arable and pasture land, and Gunvile Manor. Clearly he, his brother and his family were people of substance and standing in the town.

The story so far also raises two other questions. Was there any link between Kett's Lazar holdings and his holdings on The Lizard, the name of which is supposed to have derived from lazar house? And did Warwick - ultimately to lead the King's Army against Kett and his followers - actually know Robert and William? It is a fascinating thought.

As the hot summer of 1549 dragged on the ingredients for a major incident slowly fell into place. The West Country, a residual Catholic stronghold, suddenly reacted violently against the introduction of the New English prayerbook, seen as the final insult on top of many social injustices. In Norfolk, there was trouble at Attleborough, Eccles and Wilby, based (Dennis Chaplin) on lingering resentment over enclosures, and more particularly, on localised ineptitudes engendered "between competing gentry and between gentry and smallholders."

At Wymondham, local loudmouths may have been searching for an excuse for some sort of confrontation. Perhaps it was a case of "anything Attleborough can do we can do better." In any event the town was already seething with rumour and resentment over the abbey church affair. It needed only a large gathering and the lax application of public order regulations for tempers to burst through.

As for Robert Kett, his bag of resentment was overflowing. He may have echoed guild concerns over order, decency and social justice, and expressed moral outrage at the callous disregard by some of the county landowners at the plight of the "poore commons." Or his anger may have been fuelled by the provocative action of his old rival, Flowerdew, the demolition of the abbey and the threats to the parish church and Becket's chapel. Perhaps Kett saw Flowerdew as a man busily blunting his own business opportunities, and a local rising, with himself as leader, as a last avenue for fame and notoriety. But Kett at 57, whatever his energy and determination, was hardly a young adventurer. Rather, he was an elderly business opportunist (though brother William may have been the wealthier of the two), comfortably off, spiritual and respected. Perhaps he genuinely felt that if there was a rising the King's Government would support reform of a largely corrupt Norfolk society.

Whatever the reasons for his ultimate involvement, the root cause must have been deep seated and genuinely felt, which suggests that the dispute over the local church could been an overriding factor.

On Saturday, July 6, 1549, noisy crowds gathered in Wymondham for the annual Feast of St Thomas of Canterbury. It was a much-loved event, two days and a night packed with celebration and festivity, mystery plays, processions, pageants, eating, drinking and merriment; a

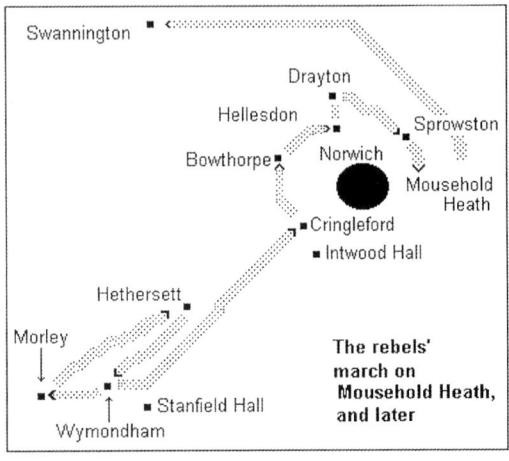

relief, no doubt, from the harsh realities of everyday life. And this time it seems to have been blessed with hot, dry weather, entirely conducive to long hours outside. There is a slight suggestion that this may also have been an illegal gathering, for Henry V111 had erased Thomas's name from the Christian calendar and abolished guilds dedicated to the martyr. In any event Wymondham liked the fair, and it liked Becket. And no doubt the excitement, heat, colour, noise and beer eventually had an effect, leaving the town seething with suppressed tension.

On Monday, July 8, and as if to a pre-arranged plan, the bubble finally burst when a small group of disgruntled commoners, some of them no doubt nursing thick heads, walked the three or four miles to Morley and pulled down fences which a Mr Hobart had erected around the common, then in the vicinity of Morley Manor, not far from the present school.

So far most of the Norfolk protests, aside from Castle Rising, and Suffolk incidents in Bungay and Beccles, had been concentrated in a swathe of countryside south-west of Wymondham, suggesting either copycat actions or a degree of collusion. At this point, however, the rioters did something quite out of character. Instead of dispersing and going home they wandered all or part of the way from Morley to Hethersett (another nine miles or so) evidently bent on attacking fences erected by the unpopular Flowerdew.

The lawyer was ready for them. Perhaps forewarned, he confronted the rioters before they could do their work, distributed between them what now seems the paltry sum of 40 pence - suggesting the gathering was relatively small - and somehow convinced them they would be doing much more worthwhile work if they turned around and attacked the fences of one Robert Kett which enclosed a

Wymondham common. This enclosure is thought to have joined or been in the vicinity of Fairland. And this they did. But here was the second surprise of the day. Kett listened to their grievances, sided with them, and actually helped them in their task. Then - and he must have enjoyed this - he led them back to Hethersett again, this time to complete the job against Flowerdew's fences.

By my calculation this would have made a total of upwards of 20 miles of aimless traipsing (though they may, of course, have ridden), a great many by today's softer standards but probably a comparatively small expedition for a bunch of 16th century commoners toughened by outdoor work and buoyed by beer and bravado.

But the day had something even more extraordinary to offer. At some point after the group returned from Hethersett, or perhaps during the night, Kett evidently agreed to become their leader, and more,

Kett's Oak, near Hethersett.

agreed that he would lead them to Norwich. Holinshed says he "willed them to be of good comfort and to follow him in defence of their common liberty." Kett may have realised that, with Government troops already in action in the West Country he was stretching official lines of communication to the limit and that it would take London a long time to do anything about it. In fact, as An Historical Atlas of Norfolk points out, the policy of the Norfolk protesters seems to have been to make camp near local centres of administration.

Whatever the reasons behind his decision, and the timing of it, next day, Tuesday, July 9, found the mob swelled by other protesters newly arrived from surrounding areas. Then, presumably during the morning, they set off along the old Norwich road towards Hethersett, pausing at a large oak tree whose site on the former A11 road is now remembered by the name, Kett's Oak.

Scrawny and frail, propped by timbers and held together by iron ribbing, this old tree can only hint at its former glory. Rosemary Tilbrook (EDP, January, 1994) has described it as a pedunculate oak in "late middle age." In 1841 it was said to have been some 9ft in circumference and "reduced to a shell of its former glory." Stakes and an iron band were in use even then. Four years later White's Norfolk directory also described it as "decayed" and "hooped and screwed together." To have been a tree of size and significance in 1549, the tree you see today would have to be in the region of 500 years old. It is a tantalising thought.

Incidentally, this tree must not be confused with another also made famous by the episode and now disappeared, the so-called Oak of Reformation, on the former Mousehold Heath at Thorpe Hamlet, Norwich, or with another Kett's Oak at Ryston, which is said to mark the spot where the Castle Rising rebels camped on their way to Mousehold.

Whatever the truth, some writers say it was under the Hethersett oak that Kett and his rapidly swelling large band of followers took a solemn oath to reform the abuses of Church and State, and it might have been under this tree they also took the decision to march to Norwich. In the event the mob passed through Hethersett, crossed the river Yare at Cringleford and turned left towards Bowthorpe, where they made camp after a presumably exciting and exhausting day.

It is not clear if the reason for the Bowthorpe move was because Norwich had denied them a right of passage through the city. What is clear is that the city fathers, seeing the size of the gathering and not unnaturally alarmed, hurriedly sent appeals for help to the local gentry and to the King at Windsor. And in what looked like a plea for moderation and a delaying tactic, the mayor of Norwich, Thomas Codd - who seems to have favoured a firm but moderate approach - and other leading citizens, rode to the camp to plead with the rioters to disperse. They met with no success. Instead, some of the excited gathering demonstrated their confidence by taking advantage of the lull to pull down fences in a city close.

Next day, Wednesday, July 10, the camp received another important visitor who also pleaded with them to disperse. This time it was Sir Edward Wyndham, of Felbrigg, the High Sheriff of Norfolk who, despite his office, received almost as short shrift as Mayor Codd. Wyndham, presumably because he had no troops with him, returned to Norwich, whereupon the rebels upped camp and marched to Eaton woods.

This decision seems to suggest either they were awaiting reinforcements or that at this stage they had no plan other than to progress through the city, or perhaps reach Mousehold Heath via the city, presumably voicing their protests as they went. In the event their requests for safe passage through the streets were understandably refused by city elders who now feared the worst.

Kett did not hesitate. On July 11 the throng crossed the river Wensum at Hellesdon and moved to Drayton, where there occurred yet another curious episode, this time involving Sir Roger Wodehouse of Kimberley. He arrived on the scene with a cart load of provisions and two cart loads of beer, presumably wanting to talk to Kett, whom he may have known, and to buy off Kett's increasingly confident followers. Whether what happened next was on Kett's instructions is not clear. Perhaps it was done despite him. In any event the rebels took possession of the beer and food, chased and stripped Sir Roger and took him prisoner.

Next day the boisterous horde moved to Sprowston, where they destroyed a dovecote belonging to a lawyer, John Corbet, and did other damage, and finally reached Mousehold Heath where they requisitioned the Earl of Surrey's house (Mount Surrey) and incarcerated their prisoners, presumably including Wodehouse and possibly including two men named Gawdy, who may have been the Recorder of Lynn, and an MP, and Catlyn, and two brothers from Stanfield Hall who evidently had connections with Flowerdew. The taking of prisoners and the making of a prison helps to underline the oft repeated point that a certain level of planning and policy-making must have taken place quite early in the affair.

The question of pre-planning raises a number of questions. How widespread was the rebellion? Had the Wymondham rioters simply been awaiting a signal? Perhaps the missing ingredient was a leader, a gap which was not plugged until Kett arrived on the scene, whereupon everything fell into place. In any event, hindsight seems to suggest that with all the issues and grievances in place it was a rising waiting to happen, and that had it not occurred in 1549 it might have happened in 1550 or 1551.

All that is known as far as Norfolk is concerned is that there were rebel camps at Castle Rising, Downham Market, Watton and Hingham in addition to Mousehold, and that there was serious fighting at Sprowston and Norwich. Incidents and skirmishes were also recorded at Lynn, Thetford, Kenninghall, New Buckenham, Hingham, Morley, Wymondham, Hethersett, Eaton, Costessey, Hellesdon, Sprowston and Yarmouth. A further indication of the level of support for Kett is that rebels from nearly 50 parishes are known to have taken part, most of them evenly spread throughout the county with the possible exception of the north-east and the south-west.

The next question is: how many rebels were there? Traditionally, it is claimed that 20,000 camped on the Heath, but modern writers seem to prefer a more modest total somewhere between 10,000 and 15,000. In any event, and by the rule of the day, it was a huge and threatening gathering, and it is easy to understand why a fearful Norwich held its breath. Clearly, some city inhabitants supported the aims of the rebels. But for the next few weeks city officials, tradesmen and gentry must have slept very uneasily, if they slept at all.

If Kett's first plan was simply to put on a show of strength and win over hearts and minds in Norwich, then his selection of a site for the camp on the heath could not have been bettered. In Kett's day (Goreham) this huge tract of woodland and uncultivated land had a perimeter of about 22 miles and stretched from the outskirts of Norwich almost as far as Woodbastwick and Ranworth, bordering Sprowston and Salhouse to the north and Little Plumstead to the south. It was important to the local economy in a number of ways, one being that surrounding villages turned out their sheep and cattle, as was their right, on "free Musholde."

Beyond the fortified Bishop's Gate (known as Holmestrete) bridge, on the east side of the river, was a patch of open meadow crossed by a track, an old Roman road, which straggled up a steep incline now known as Gas Hill. On both sides of this road the heath thrust upwards and formed a precipitous escarpment which, then as now, towers over the eastern environs of the city.

There were many reasons for digging in here. First, it was a position of stragetic impregnability and one from which Kett could dominate Norwich with his cannon. Second, it provided a brooding presence, gave close access to the city, and placed a military wedge between Norwich and the port of Yarmouth. Third, there was open country on three sides, giving access to farms and villages, and thus supplies, should they not be available from the city itself. Fourth, of course, it afforded the rebels a perfect view not only of the bridge and river but also of much of the city. Scarcely a soldier could move in the streets without being spotted by look-outs on the heath.

Interestingly, subsequent events revealed a fifth reason, namely, the fact the camp also overlooked one of the weakest parts of the city's defences and was thus a useful platform for launching assaults. Aside from fortifications at the bridge, the city walls did not extend along the riverbank, which meant they could be out flanked by anyone wading, swimming or boating over the Wensum in the vicinity of what is now the Norwich School playing fields or the meadows near Cow Tower, anciently known as the Dungeon or Hassets Tower.

On the right up the hill stood St Leonard's Priory, which once covered 24 acres. Geoffrey Goreham (see below) writes that the priory may have been named after St Leonard, a French noble (died AD559) who is thought to have built himself a hut in nearby woods to live a life of devotion. The priory was a cell to and dependent on the cathedral monastery. In 1538 the site of the old priory was granted to Thomas, Duke of Norfolk, whose son, Henry Howard, Earl of Surrey, built a house there. Nine years later, when the Earl was beheaded, the property reverted to the Crown, and it was this building which Kett and his followers seized.

Not far away, too, were the ruins of St Michael's chapel which also overlooked the city and which Kett used as a watchtower. The chapel had been built outside the walls of the old priory as a replacement for St Michael, Tombland, demolished when the cathedral monastery was extended.

At the foot of the precipice, as indeed they had along much of the length of the escarpment, brave souls had burrowed into the cliffs and dug a network of tunnels and caves. There is no evidence that Kett or his followers made use of them, but caves there certainly were. Geoffrey Kelly (article, Underneath Norwich: Chalk and Flint Workings. Bulletin of the Norfolk Archaeological and Historical Research Group, No 3, 1994) points out that flint extraction workers, called stoneminers, were already busy on the heath during the 16th century, the earliest reference being 1388. Other stoneminers (1427/8, for example) also worked the heath, taking away material by the cart load.

Another site, a veritable scar on the landscape which was right under the rebels' noses, was Lollards Pit situated at the foot of the escarpment opposite Bishop's Bridge and beside the old Roman road. The name Lollard was given in the 14th and 15th centuries to, among others, the followers of John Wycliffe, the actual name

Bishopgate Bridge, Norwich, which is now closed to wheeled traffic.

being derived from the Dutch lollen, meaning to sing in an undertone. In England, use of the word was extended to cover anyone who, under a religious guise, was deemed to have "turbulent motives." Not all Lollards were followers of Wycliffe, but as a reforming group they tended to attack ecclesiastical hierarchy, clerical celibacy, the Mass, prayers for the dead, war and capital punishment, and they often charged the clergy with immorality.

Between 1401 and 1532 some 47 Lollards are said to have suffered the extreme punishment, death by burning, for heresy. The Norwich pit was certainly used in 1534, during the reign of Henry V111 and the prelacy of Richard Nykke, or Nix, Bishop of Norwich. Among others, the reformers Ayres, Bingy, Norrice and Bilney met their deaths here.

Today, the area of Thorpe Hamlet between Gas Hill and Kett's Hill still contains echoes of the King's Great Camp. Kett's Hill is an obvious reminder, and so is Camp Grove. There is also a house at the end of St Leonard's Road called Kett's

Castle Villa. The site of Mount Surrey, where Kett kept his prisoners, is now in private hands, though I believe only fragments of the original building remain. Best reminders of all, perhaps, are the sparse ruins of St Michael's chapel, in Jubilee Heights, once a mature ornamental garden belonging to managers of a nearby and subsequently demolished gas works, and now a city nature reserve accessible from Kett's Hill.

Once upon a time the chapel was about 42ft long and 18ft wide. Little has survived other than a portion of flint wall, but it is still worth the effort to climb up there, through the trees and tangled vegetation, to see something of the view that Kett and his followers saw all those years ago.

As Land has pointed out, the city fathers decided early on to establish relations with the camp, perhaps on the basis that an uneasy peace was of mutual benefit. It meant Windsor had more time to muster forces, it enabled Kett to organise his camp and formulate his plans, and while both sides held back from direct confrontation neither had to clarify their position. In reality, the relationship seems to have been somewhat complex. Rebels went into the city and citizens visited the camp. No doubt some of the residents actively aided the rebels by trading supplies. Tradesmen and gentry, increasingly concerned and alarmed by the camp and its attendant ruffians, presumably took what precautions they could including sending messages pleading for help.

They knew, and no doubt Kett suspected, that the city castle was wholly inadequate for defence and too central for the use of artillery. It did not cover the east of the city opposite Mousehold and its walls were somewhat frail. As things turned out, it played practically no role in the conflict.

Kett went about his business, apparently organising the camp as a sort of self-governing community, or seat of government. Church services were held daily despite the fact that prisoners were held in chains not far away; justice was administered, lawyers and scribes employed, warrants issued and "governors" appointed for 24 Norfolk hundreds.

Support for the camp came from individuals and from communities. Carlton Colville (Suffolk), provided money, while men from North Elmham, with their parish clerk, joined the camp, being paid 3d a day by the parish. L McMurdo (article, Norfolk Research Committee Bulletin, No 33, March, 1985) pointed out that North Elmham also engaged carriers to transport meal, meat, salt, bread, fish and onions to the camp, while arrowheads and arrows were purchased and the wives and families of some of the absent volunteers were supported with small grants of money. Licences gave suppliers access to the heath community, but a certain amount of foraging also went on.

Of course, as the weeks passed and sources of supply gradually dried up, theft and pillage increased over a large area, for the requisitioning of food for, say, 15,000 people, would have been an immense task. In the final reckoning animal and crop losses by landowners and farmers were probably enormous. According to White's Directory, provisions for a "few days" amounted to some 3000 bullocks, 20,000 sheep, corn, geese and swans, some filched, perhaps, from the swan pit at the Great Hospital, not far from Bishop's Gate bridge. At the same time, cannon was obtained from Lynn and Yarmouth, Paston Hall was forced to yield guns, and powder and arms were taken from the city.

Kett, meanwhile, held court and issued edicts sitting under what became known as the Oak of Reformation - thought to have stood roughly where the water tower in Lion Wood now stands - planks and timbers having been laid across some of the boughs to make a platform. His followers, for their part, found shelter where they could, some of them building turf and bough huts. All of which sounds like preparation for a relatively long stay.

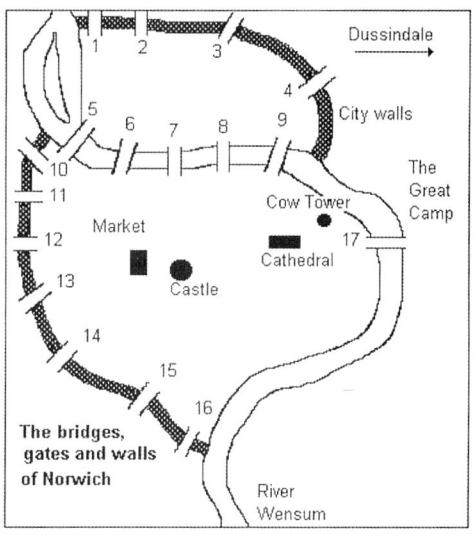

1, St Martin's; 2, St Austin's; 3, Magdalen Gate; 4, Pockthorpe; 5, New Mills; 6, Coslany; 7, Blackfriars'; 8, Fibridge; 9, Whitefriars'; 10, Heyham; 11, St Benet's; 12, St Giles; 13, St Stephen's; 14, Brasen Doors; 15, Ber Street; 16, Conisford; 17, Bishop's Bridge.

Just how long he was able to maintain discipline is a matter of conjecture, but it is hard to believe that throughout the seven weeks the camp on the heath was all sweetness and light. Indeed, there is evidence it was not. Frustration and drunkenness would have set in, bad weather, hunger and cold would have taken their toll, and it is a fair bet that among those drawn to it were unruly elements whose interests were more disruptive than reformist, just as activists are drawn to modern-day disputes.

W A Dutt (Highways & Byways in East Anglia. Macmillan, 1932) commented that at first order was preserved among the insurgents, "but their assembling led to the congregating of a host of questionable characters glad of any excuse for indulging in robbery and debauchery." White's Directory, admittedly scathingly critical of Kett and his followers, said the "county suffered under extraction and outrages," and suggested that some inhabitants were murdered. Dutt took a softer line: "Many depredations were undoubtedly committed, both in Norwich and the surrounding district; but these were probably the result of hunger or the work of the thievish rapscallions who had joined the reformers." In the end, perhaps Kett was simply unable to retain control of the forces he had unleashed.

The list of demands eventually issued from the camp and sent to the King, and presumably much influenced by Kett - the surviving manuscript is signed by Kett, Codd and Aldrich - is a curious collection of 29 paragraphs which, far from representing some unified national policy, read like a muddled list of local grievances. The largest number are about land, common rights, rents and prices; only about half a dozen relate to the priesthood.

While they do complain of ecclesiastical slackness - some priests, apparently, could not remember the Commandments, and many children did not know the catechism - the demands seemed to rule out the admittedly faint possibility that the rebellion was against Protestant reform. The evidence is heavily the other way. In any event, and had they been anti-reformist, the rebels would surely have turned to Princess Mary, the heir presumptive and a Catholic, patiently waiting at Kenninghall.

Instead, the demands contained complaints about the enclosure of saffron grounds, rents, common lands and profits, land prices and marsh rents, a plea for restrictions on the ownership of dovehouses, demands that rivers and commons should be free to all for fishing and passage, a restriction on the keeping of conies (rabbits) on commons, grumbles about inflation and a plea for a relaxation of some of the rules governing mariners and fishermen. They also demanded that all bond men should be free, that there should be a tightening of judicial and administrative processes, and a suggestion that clergy having a benefice of £10 or more should be made responsible for teaching the children of poor people the catechism and primer.

All in all not a document for the very poor, more an attempt to improve the lot of those of modest means, including small landowners.

But we are too far ahead. On July 13 the King's Herald, Grove Pursuivant, arrived in Norwich with a commission from the King to Dr Robert Watson, a popular reformist Protestant preacher, whom he no doubt hoped would be able to calm the insurgents. Watson, along with mayor Codd and the elderly, wealthy alderman Aldrich of Mangreen Hall, who may have known Kett, did indeed visit the camp to preach law and order. His advice fell on deaf ears. But at least the visit scored a small success in that the rebels were persuaded to accept Thomas Conyers, one of the "new preachers," as chaplain, who evidently gave them long Protestant sermons.

Another visitor to the camp on the same day, or perhaps the previous evening, was Matthew Parker, the Norwich-born Master of Corpus Christi College who became Archbishop of Canterbury in 1559. It was his junior secretary, Alexander

Neville, who eventually wrote an account of the Rising. Parker may have been in Norwich visiting his brother at the time of the commotion and may simply have visited the camp out of curiosity. In the event he apparently arrived in the middle of a heated debate over whether mayor Codd of Norwich should resign.

When Parker visited the camp a second time Conyers was leading prayers. Parker, at the Oak of Reformation, begged leave to address the throng and promptly made a strong plea for patience and moderation, urging the rebels to disperse. It was not what they wanted to hear, and matters became heated. Parker was jostled and had his feet pricked by pikes, and the situation was only retrieved when the quick-thinking Conyers signalled to his choristers to begin the Te Deum (in the New English fashion). The crowd joined in and a no doubt relieved Parker slipped away.

Much chastened, he seems to have rushed back into the city and promptly preached against the rebellion in several churches, including St Clements, where his parents were buried. Then, according to Ravensdale & Muir, some rebel supporters in one of the congregations, who may have been in the city requisitioning supplies, warned him his horses were to be taken. Parker rapidly had them doctored to appear lame. Next day, July 15, he walked to Cringleford, where fresh horses were waiting, and slipped away to the safety of Cambridge.

Monday, July 15, also saw the start of a six-day lull which, nevertheless, was to have a considerable effect on the great commotion. At some point prominent Norwich citizen Leonard Sotherton (the brother of Nicholas, who wrote an eye witness account of the revolt) also slipped out of the city to make the long journey to London. He eventually appeared before the King's Council to plead for assistance for the city, only to be told, bluntly, that no forces were available. Most of them were deployed in the West Country. Someone then suggested that the offer of a pardon should be made to the rebels, and with this one slim weapon in his pocket, and accompanied by York Herald, Sotherton rode back to Norwich.

York Herald visited the city council chamber on July 21 and then, accompanied by the City Sword bearer, visited the camp and relayed the offer of a pardon. Some of the rebels were evidently receptive, but the majority turned it down. Oddly, the Herald then ordered the Sword bearer, one John Petibone, to arrest the rebels - which was rather like Custer ordering one of his officers to arrest the Indians - a task quite beyond even Mr Petibone. So the official party returned down the hill, re-entering the city across the Bishop's Gate bridge.

It was a turning point. Before July 21, Kett's main considerations were administration of the camp, the maintenance of discipline, and demands for reform. Now he and his followers were set firmly outside of the law. Their actions were an affront to the King. If they continued on this path then it was only a question of time before troops would be sent.

In Norwich, mayor Codd must also have weighed the situation. At least he knew where Kett stood. The days of moderation and grudging co-operation were at an end. He ordered the city gates to be closed, the walls to be manned, lookouts to be posted and cannon placed on the river meadows beside Bishop's Gate bridge. Kett's men watched the preparations from on high and promptly hauled their guns on to the high ground of the heath. Before darkness fell a desultory exchange of fire broke out. Less than two weeks had passed since the march to Norwich had begun.

Fighting began in earnest on July 22. Kett asked for safe passage into the city to provision his army, but the request was refused. This time an intense artillery duel broke out. Then the rebels attempted to storm Bishop's Gate bridge, but were halted by archers and had to resort to the expedient of swimming the river to outflank the defensive positions. Once inside the city the rebels poured through the narrow streets, commandeering guns and powder as they went. York Herald, standing in front of a noisy crowd in the market place, attempted to re-read the offer of a pardon, but was howled down.

Thus for a week or so Kett lived a dual existence, that of commandant of the city and leader of the rebels. The camp on the heath was maintained, perhaps because he realised the city could not be defended against a large force, and prisoners, including mayor Codd, preacher Watson and some aldermen, were clapped in irons and dragged off to Mount Surrey. The affairs of the city were taken over by the deputy mayor, Augustine Steward.

By July 29 Kett knew that Government forces were on the way. Under the command of the Marquis of Northampton (Sir William Parr, the brother of Catherine Parr and a supporter of Somerset), a woefully inadequate contingent of about 1500 troops, including some Italian

A view of Bishopgate and the Cathedral, Norwich, from the site of the Great Camp.

mercenaries, nevertheless managed to subdue a rebel camp at Bury St Edmunds. On July 31 they arrived on the outskirts of Norwich. Kett's men withdrew to the heath and Northampton entered the city unopposed. Perhaps against his instinct - he was heavily out-numbered, remember - Northampton seems to have decided the city would have to be defended, and he set labourers to work repairing the damaged gates.

It was a curious decision because it left him in a difficult defensive position with his modest forces thinly spread. Then there was the embarrassing matter of the Italians, a group of whom accidently strayed outside the city limits right under the noses of the rebels. They came under immediate attack and an officer was captured. Dragged back to the heath, the unfortunate foreigner was promptly hanged. Even so, York Herald was again disposed read the offer of a pardon once more, this time outside Pockthorpe gates, only to see it rejected yet again. Kett, perhaps sensing the frailty of Northampton's position, promptly bombarded the city.

After a night of heavy firing the rebels again attacked Bishop's Gate bridge and this time broke into what is now called Bishopgate and into St Martin-at-Palace Plain. The ferocious fighting lasted until noon, and between 40 and 140 are believed to have been killed, including Lord Sheffield and several of Northampton's lieutenants. Many others were wounded and houses and buildings damaged and set on fire. The constant bombardment also led to the partial destruction of Cow Tower, dating from 1398/9. Brian Ayres (Norwich. English Heritage, 1994) recorded that traces of burning still exist at the top of the tower. Bishop's Gate bridge was certainly damaged, along with buildings on the Common Staithe and at the Great Hospital, while Whitefriars' bridge is said to have been demolished. The flames were not dowsed until a heavy downpour of rain swept across the city, but by this time Northampton had already withdrawn. Like Parker, he decided to seek safety in Cambridge.

Instead of moving back to the heath, Kett, this time in complete charge and with no Government troops in the area, set up a garrison camp in the grounds of the cathedral and took over the running of the city.

There is no doubt he also tried to widen the scope of the rising. A rebel camp at Melton evidently accepted an offer of a pardon, but others at Watton and Hingham moved to Norwich to join the main force. The camp at Castle Rising also attempted to move, but the rebels found themselves under constant attack from gentry including Sir Edward Knyvett, of New Buckenham castle. And in what at this distance seems a ludicrous move, the rebels also attempted to storm the port of Yarmouth. It was a military disaster. They fired haystacks to create a smoke screen, but the town captured 30 rebels and six guns.

Supplies were becoming increasingly difficult to obtain, reinforcements were having difficulty in getting through, and Kett's main force was to all intents and purposes on its own.

To add to their difficulties, though Kett may not have known it at the time, the task of defeating the rebels was being given to the Earl of Warwick whose force, while still outnumbered, is thought initially to have been in the region of 6000, including 1500 horsemen. On August 21 Warwick joined forces with Northampton at Cambridge. At Lynn, Lord Willoughby also assembled troops ostensibly to march on the other rebel centres. Perhaps because these particular threats had largely evaporated, Willoughby changed his tactics and seems to have joined forces with Warwick.

The force left Cambridge and marched through Newmarket and Thetford, arriving at Wymondham on August 22. What a spectacle that must have been, and what savage ironies were brought into play! Two days later, as yet more Government reinforcements arrived, Warwick set up his headquarters at the Intwood Hall home of Sir Thomas Gresham.

It is not clear where all the local reinforcements came from, but Ben Ripper (Ribbons from the Pedlar's Pack. Daedalus Press, 1979) recorded a Swaffham church account of 1553 which stated: "Item for harness, horse and money, 20 men to go about the King's business at commotion time." The money, borrowed from various people in the parish who were evidently repaid when the church plate was sold, amounted to £50 11s. Ripper also suggested that about 20 men of the Swaffham contingent did not return from the final battle, and that there were probably Swaffham men on both sides of the military divide on Mousehold Heath.

Later, a band of German mercenary lancers would also arrive, so that at a final count Warwick may have had somewhere between 8000 and 14,000 hard-bitten professional troops at his disposal.

Warwick seems to have made yet another effort to avoid a confrontation, asking Norroy Herald, Gilbert Dethick, to order the city to receive his troops. Kett, who seems to have been in the city at the time, and hearing of the Herald's appearance at St Stephen's Gate, persuaded Augustine Steward, the deputy mayor, and Robert Rugge, a former mayor, to conduct the parley on his behalf. This pair, not unnaturally, suggested that the offer of pardon - which specifically excluded Kett - be repeated.

It would be interesting to know if Kett knew they would do this; in any event Warwick promptly agreed. The Herald was then admitted to the city on Kett's orders and escorted to Bishop's Gate bridge. A trumpeter called rebels from the camp on the heights of Mousehold, and a huge crowd gathered.

Sotherton says the mood was one of good humour, but the undiplomatic Dethick seems to have put his foot in it by accusing the rebels of treason and threatening them with Warwick's army if they did not comply with the conditions of the pardon. There was uproar. The Herald was verbally abused though Kett, apparently arriving late on the scene, managed to calm matters and moved him a short distance from Bishop's Gate bridge.

Kett asked him to read the offer a second time. There then occurred yet another of those curious incidents which litter the history of the rebellion. As the Herald was reading the offer of the pardon a small boy, presumably overcome with excitement and bravado, turned and exposed his buttocks to the Herald. He was promptly killed by one of the Herald's entourage, and this time the angry mood of the crowd spilled over. Amid uproar, Kett and the Herald's party retreated inside the city.

Kett's intentions at this point are unclear. Why did he arrive late at the reading of the pardon? Was it deliberate, or was he prevented from doing so? Had he by this time lost control of the situation and was he simply being swept along by events? Certainly he did his best to protect the Herald and extricate him from the mob. What happened after the Herald and Kett left the scene seems to suggest that some sort of solution was in the air. A group of rebels rode after Kett and the Herald, halted them, and asked Kett why he was going away.

It seems likely that Kett, recognising the whole enterprise was entering its final phase, was hoping to meet Warwick face to face perhaps to negotiate a pardon for himself as well as his followers. If so, then he may have been at odds with more militant factions at the camp. He may also have been physically prevented from talking to Warwick. Whatever the underlying reasons, Kett stayed with the rebels and the Herald returned to Intwood Hall. Negotiations were at an end.

When Warwick finally unsheathed his troops they promptly broke through the portcullis at St Stephen's Gate, seized Brazen Gates and took advantage of the fact that Augustine Steward had arranged for St Benedict's Gates to be opened. Bitter street fighting continued through the afternoon of August 24 until Warwick's

Augustine Steward's house in Tombland.

men finally smashed their way through to the market place, hanging nearly 50 captured rebels on the spot. Kett's men seem to have rallied and established a bridgehead in the Tombland and Bishop's Gate area and then counter-attacked from three points - St Michael at Plea, Elm Hill, and near St Andrew's Hall. Warwick himself led a ferocious reply, the fighting being prolonged and desperate, and the King's men slowly gained control. Eventually the rebels withdrew but Kett's gunners, using captured ordnance, continued to pound Bishop's Gate and the eastern defences.

Militarily, at least, the combatants had reached some sort of stalemate. But John Dudley, the Earl of Warwick, was a seasoned soldier, battle-hardened by the French campaigns of Henry Vlll. He was also a champion of wealth and property and a man with political ambition, so he may well have seen the rebellion as an opportunity to enhance and enlarge his own stature. If he had wanted to be known as a strong man with a "no nonsense" approach in dealing with malcontents, then here was the ideal opportunity. Of course, he was also the man who had had business dealings with Kett in the past.

Common sense must have warned him the city could not be defended against determined attackers. He had proved it himself that very morning, and Kett had proved it on several occasions, mainly to the discomfort of Northumberland. First, Warwick was out-numbered and the rebels held the higher and better ground. Second, he was vulnerable to counter-attack. The city population was divided, the walls and perimeter could be breached, and he and his troops were at a disadvantage if they were drawn into hand to hand fighting in the maze of narrow streets.

If he needed further confirmation of the problem then the loss of an ammunition and ordnance supply train - which occurred when baggage-masters took a wrong turning and guided the stores right into the arms of the rebels - must have provided it. He must have suspected that a set-piece battle on open ground was his best chance, even if there was no certainty he would win.

Robert Kett and his advisors may have realised this, too. They may also have realised their options were running out and that the longer they could keep Warwick cooped up in the city the better. Perhaps with this in mind, on Sunday, August 25, the rebels again swarmed down from the heath and launched another ferocious and highly organised attack, this time against Bishop's Gate and Conisford. At some point during the morning, as Warwick was breakfasting at Augustine Steward's house, some of the rebels broke through into what is now King Street, starting fires and causing untold damage.

Somewhat unexpectedly, and in what seems to have been a refinement of their tactics, they also broke through between Magdalen and Pockthorpe Gates. In both cases, and after heavy fighting and mounting losses on both sides, Warwick checked the advance and this time ordered the destruction of several bridges as a means of slowing any new attack on his lines. He set up his arms (bear and ragged staff) on Augustine Steward's house in Tombland and considered the situation. The timely arrival, on Monday, August 26, of a large detachment of German mercenaries, some with their wives, must have been a boost to Warwick's morale even if the residents dreaded the possibility of even greater damage to property and person.

Kett would also have known that Warwick's reinforcements had arrived, and may have watched them from one of the viewpoints on the heath. He knew resistance in the city was stiffening. There were surely other problems, too. The condition of the camp, after seven long weeks of activity, must have been appalling. In addition, if the city was closed to them, if Yarmouth was still hostile, and if rebel camps elsewhere had largely disappeared from the scene, then supplies must have been increasingly difficult to obtain. Militarily, too, the rebel position was not as overwhelming as it had been. They had already lost a lot of men and there was the possibility that Warwick's rejuvenated forces might try to launch some sort of flanking attack to push them off the heights and trap them against the marshes and the sea.

Of course, it is not known if Kett was still in complete control. The incident with the Herald could well have left an aftertaste with the more militant rebel factions. Some groups, no doubt, had favoured acceptance of a pardon, believing they had done as much for the cause as they could. Others might have sensed a trap, or would have wanted to fight to the bitter end. Quite what discussions went on that day will never be known, but two overriding ingredients, in the end, probably flavoured the decision: the camp on the heath was coming to an end, and the chance of a pardon had gone. Two old rhyming prophecies, however, may have given them heart:

"The country gnoffes
Hob, Dick and Hick,
With clubs and clouted shoon
Shall fill the vale of Dussindale
With slaughtered bodies soon."
and
"The heedless men within the dale
Shall there be slain both great and small."

The origin and meaning of the verses is obscure, but Sotherton commented sourly that instead of putting their trust in God the rebels "trustid uppon faynid prophecies which were phantastically devisid . . . " The implication is that the verses were interpreted as speaking of victory for the rebels. Whatever the precise reasons, sometime on that Monday in August, when most of Kett's followers would normally have been immersed in nothing more harmful than harvest operations, they took the decision to provoke the final, decisive confrontation.

With Warwick still outnumbered the rebels may have been confident of victory. But such matters are not clear cut, as Boudica also discovered when her numerically superior force found itself in a set-piece battle against a small, disciplined army led by a wily campaigner. In the event, and some time after dark, Warwick's lookouts in the city reported seeing fires and large scale rebel movements on the heath. Preparations for the last act were in hand.

The decision to fire the camp may have been to add a touch of finality to the matter, a last piece of drama, suggesting they were unconcerned at the prospect of Warwick being alerted. What it did underline was that the night manoeuvres were designed to give them time to complete preparations, rather than hide their intentions. Warwick, despite the alert, could do little until daybreak.

Early attempts to resolve the location of Dussindale tended to place it roughly in the area

The ruins of St Michael's Chapel on Jubilee Heights, off Kett's Hill.

between Rosebury and Albany roads. It is known, for example, that Warwick's troops eventually crossed Coslany bridge and left the city by way of St Martin's Gate. Nevill said the name was long lost, but the site was then (1857) known as Home Valley and ran at the rear of the barracks between Magdalen Hill and Denmark Lane. He said Silver Road, from Pockthorpe to Rackheath, passed through Home Valley. Land, who pointed out that the final indictment against Kett placed the incident in the parishes of Sprowston and Thorpe, thought the most likely site was outside the city walls to the north-east.

Studies by Anne Carter have fuelled the debate even further. Researching the history of Postwick, she came across a number of references to Dussindale which would have placed it about two miles east of Mount Surrey on the boundaries of Thorpe St Andrew, Postwick and Great Plumstead. Her references included Dussings Dale (early 18th century), Dussings Deale (1718), Dussinges Dale (1576) and Dussinge Dale (1652). Superimposed on a modern map, Dussindale would have followed the course of Green Lane south from Low Road to the A47.

Kett's men evidently used what time was available to them by building some sort of defensive position on the open heath, digging trenches and bulwarks, positioning stakes and, says Land, placing "their ordnance all about them." They also brought up their prisoners - some of whom had escaped and fled back to the city - chained them together and positioned them in the front rank, presumably to intimidate and confuse Warwick's gunners.

Warwick's instinct would have told him this was the decisive moment, his chance to break free of the shackles of the city streets. When his troops finally marched out of St Martin's Gate, and providing the Postwick location of Dussindale is correct, then they would have faced a relatively easy march across the heath. Faden's Map of Norfolk, 1797 (Larks Press, 1989) shows a road of less than two miles linking Kett's Castle ruins with Thorpe Farm at the northern end of the presumed Dussindale. Another route, roughly up the present Kett's Hill and along Yarmouth Road, would have taken them to the other end of the dale.

In any event, it was now possible that upwards of 25,000 men faced each other across the great divide. There must have been a sharp intake of breath when the final offer of a pardon - which again excluded the leaders - was rejected.

An early move seems to have been by Kett's master gunner, Miles, who killed the Royal standard bearer. Then Warwick's cavalry charged, and after much frantic fighting the rebel lines wobbled; mercenary harquebusiers (an arquebus was a long-barrelled gun fired by wheel-lock or matchlock), pouring fire into the hubbub, finally broke the rebel lines. In the confusion the prisoners escaped, apparently unscathed.

It quickly turned into a rout, Kett's force becoming fragmented. One group prepared to make a last stand behind a barricade of wagons, whereupon Warwick made yet another attempt to end the slaughter. He sent a herald to repeat the offer of a pardon, and this time the rebels said they would accept if Warwick himself appeared on the scene. He did, and he confirmed the promise, and at four o'clock on the afternoon of Tuesday, August 27, the fighting died away. Later reports suggested that Warwick may have lost 250 men, the rebels in the region of 3000.

The inevitable executions soon began, some writers claiming that 300 rebels were hung and some of the leaders hanged, drawn and quartered. A few of the executions took place at the Oak of Reformation; some other of the dead were buried outside Magdalen Gate. On Warwick's side the losses included Robert

Knyvett, Thomas Wodehouse, a priest, and six others, who were all buried at St Peter Mancroft in Norwich.

W A Dutt (Highways & Byways in East Anglia. Macmillan, 1932) wrote that the register of burials at St Simon's church included Henry Wilby, Gyles ffoster and Thomas Lyusye, all from Warwickshire, and Lusonn, of North Hampton. The entry, he said, read: "Thes 4 esquires weare slayne in the King's army on Mushold Heath, the Tewestaye being the xxvijtie daye of August, 1549, anno tertio Edwardi Sexti, and were all buryed in the chauncell of this church in one grave." The city Chamberlain's list of market stalls (Green & Young. Norwich, the Growth of a City. Norfolk Museums Service, 1981) showed several vacancies because the tenants had joined the rebels, fled, or had been executed. Meanwhile, loyal citizens and returning soldiery celebrated in the streets and services of thanksgiving were held in the churches.

Sometime before this, Kett, seeing the day was lost, had slipped quietly away from the battlefield. Sotherton suggested that Kett left the area before the fighting started, accompanied by five or six other rebels, though there does not seem to be much evidence to back this.

Whether his wandering was aimless, or whether he had some plan to reach one of North Norfolk's busy ports - Lynn or Wells, perhaps, or even Wiveton, Blakeney or Cley - is not known. By evening of August 27, however, he had reached Swannington, about 10 miles away. His dream ended, his army destroyed and his horse exhausted, he was understandably tired, doubtless having been up all the previous night, and he stopped to rest in a barn. Then some men unloading hay from a cart recognised him and took him to the house of one Master Richards, or Riches. According to the writer of The Hidden Places of Norfolk & Suffolk (Maps Marketing Ltd., 1989) this house was Swannington Hall, the oldest part of which possibly dates to the 15th century.

Here Kett fed and rested and was held until a detachment of troops arrived to take him away. Evidently resigned to his fate, he seems to have made no move to escape. Indeed, there is a story that he was even left at the house with only a small child for company while someone went for help.

Warwick stayed in the area for about ten days, settling disputes - there were plenty of them, for the gentry and citizens of Norwich were much out of pocket over the affair - and dealing with administrative matters. It was during this period that Warwick's son, Robert, is thought to have met and fallen in love with Amy Robsart. On September 7, however, Warwick left for London, taking Robert and William Kett with him. They were imprisoned in the Tower.

The trial of the brothers finally opened on Tuesday, November 26, 1549, and it did not last long. Both men pleaded guilty and offered no defence. They were sentenced accordingly. They were to be taken from the Tower to Tyburn, partially

The GREAT COMMOTION

The official plaque on the wall of Norwich Castle.

hanged, then to have their entrails taken out and burned before them, and their heads cut off and bodies quartered.

For some reason this did not take place because someone evidently decided justice must be seen to be done and that the executions should take place in Norfolk. So Robert and William were carted all the way back, perhaps being exhibited briefly in Wymondham, before being presented to the Sheriff of Norfolk, Sir Edmund Wyndham, on November 29. He took them to Norwich where Robert, at least, was chained in the Guildhall dungeon.

At some point William was taken back to Wymondham where, on December 7, he was hanged from the west tower of the Abbey. That same day Robert Kett was drawn on a hurdle through the streets of Norwich to the castle, where a rope was placed around his neck and where, still in chains, he was hoisted alive from the ground to a gibbet on top of the castle. His body was left dangling until it rotted. A mere five months had passed since the first, fateful march to Norwich.

Following the departure of the King's troops the city began to count the cost and repair the damage. There is evidence the affair was also followed by a scarcity of goods and a rise in prices, for shortly afterwards the city corporation issued an edict requiring all wealthy citizens to provide corn for their own households so the poor could have exclusive use of the city market. But in a sense there was even worse to come. Two years after the revolt a "sweating sickness" which "ended or mended" in 24 hours is said to have killed 960 people in Norwich in a few days. And by 1557 the burnings at Lollards Pit had started all over again.

The Kett Rebellion remains a paradox. It seems to have been spontaneous yet showed traces of planning and organisation. Its leader was an encloser and a minor manorial lord who claimed to uphold Government policy. It may have been a class war - peasant farmers and small tradesmen against landowners, lawyers and merchants - and yet the rebels clearly displayed a sense of community and unity.

At the very least Kett seems to have represented a glimpse of better things, though in the end the vision ran out of energy. It had no-where to go; there was nothing to nurture it. It was a case of surrender or be destroyed and, just like the revolt of Boudica, another example of "nearly, but not quite."

SELECTED REFERENCES AND READING

Carter, Anne, article. Norfolk Archaeology, Vol 34, pt 1. Norfolk & Norwich Archaeological Society, 1984.
Chaplin, Dennis. EDP (articles). July 7 and August 30, 1984.
Frere, Bartle. Amy Robsart of Wymondham. Jarrold & Sons, 1937.
Goreham, Geoffrey. Mousehold, A Short History. Mousehold Heath Defenders' booklet, undated.
Goreham, Geoffrey. Thorpe Hamlet. Thorpe Hamlet Association, 1972.
Hoare, Adrian & Anne. On the Trail of Robert Kett of Wymondham. Wymondham Society, 1985.
Hoare, Adrian. In Search of Robert Kett. Hoare, undated.
Land, Stephen. Kett's Rebellion. Boydell, 1977.
Nevill, Rev Henry. Kett's Castle, a lecture. Pamphlet printed by Thomas Priest, Norwich. 1857.
Ravensdale & Muir. East Anglian Landscapes. Joseph, 1984.
Sotherton, Nicholas. The Commoyson in Norfolk (edited by Susan Yaxley). Larks Press, 1987.
Wade-Martins, P. An Historical Atlas of Norfolk. Norfolk Museums Service, 1993.
White's 1845 Norfolk. David & Charles reprint, 1969.

PLACES TO VISIT

Start at Wymondham. The abbey church, market place, Heritage Museum, town sign, Becket's chapel (now the town library) and the bridge over the Tiffey at

Becketswell close by where Kett is thought to have lived, can all be seen. Kett's Oak can be seen beside the old A11 half way between Wymondham and Hethersett.

In Norwich, and aside from the plaque near the main entrance to the Castle Museum, there is the cathedral and the Close, Augustine Steward's house in Tombland, Bishopgate and Bishopgate bridge (though the fortified gateway has gone), Cow Tower, and the surviving pieces of St Michael's chapel on Jubilee Heights, off Kett's Hill.